Mastering
ARTIFICIAL INTELLIGENCE
AND MACHINE LEARNING
Concepts, Techniques, and Applications

Nikhilesh Mishra,
Author

Website
www.nikhileshmishra.com

Copyright Information

Copyright © 2023 Nikhilesh Mishra

Dedication

This book is lovingly dedicated to the cherished memory of my father, **Late Krishna Gopal Mishra**, and my mother**, Mrs. Vijay Kanti Mishra.** Their unwavering support, guidance, and love continue to inspire me.

Table of Contents

Author's Preface

Welcome to the captivating world of the knowledge we are about to explore! Within these pages, we invite you to embark on a journey that delves into the frontiers of information and understanding.

Charting the Path to Knowledge

Dive deep into the subjects we are about to explore as we unravel the intricate threads of innovation, creativity, and problem-solving. Whether you're a curious enthusiast, a seasoned professional, or an eager learner, this book serves as your gateway to gaining a deeper understanding.

Your Guiding Light

From the foundational principles of our chosen field to the advanced frontiers of its applications, we've meticulously crafted this book to be your trusted companion. Each chapter is an expedition, guided by expertise and filled with practical insights to empower you on your quest for knowledge.

What Awaits You

- **Illuminate the Origins:** Embark on a journey through the historical evolution of our chosen field, discovering key milestones that have paved the way for breakthroughs.

- **Demystify Complex Concepts:** Grasp the fundamental principles, navigate intricate concepts, and explore practical applications.

- **Mastery of the Craft:** Equip yourself with the skills and knowledge needed to excel in our chosen domain.

Your Journey Begins Here

As we embark on this enlightening journey together, remember that mastery is not just about knowledge but also the wisdom to apply it. Let each chapter be a stepping stone towards unlocking your potential, and let this book be your guide to becoming a true connoisseur of our chosen field.

So, turn the page, delve into the chapters, and immerse yourself in the world of knowledge. Let curiosity be your compass, and let the pursuit of understanding be your guide.

Begin your expedition now. Your quest for mastery awaits!

Sincerely,

Nikhilesh Mishra,

Author

Nikhilesh Misha

Part I

Introduction to Artificial Intelligence and Machine Learning

CHAPTER 1

Foundations of AI and Machine Learning

In the boundless expanse of human ingenuity, a new frontier has emerged – one where the realm of computation collides with the aspirations of artificial intelligence and machine learning. The foundations of AI and machine learning, meticulously woven from mathematical intricacies and cognitive paradigms, stand as the modern-day Rosetta Stone, deciphering the language of data and unraveling the enigmas of our digital universe. This captivating symphony of algorithms and insights orchestrates a dance between human intellect and silicon prowess, transmuting raw information into a tapestry of predictive prowess and automated acumen. Join us on a journey through the crystalline labyrinths of neural networks, the artistry of feature engineering, and the symphonic convergence of statistics and logic, as we embark upon an odyssey into the very bedrock of intelligent machines.

A. Definition and scope of AI and machine learning

In an era where the boundaries between science fiction and reality have blurred, Artificial Intelligence (AI) and Machine

Learning (ML) emerge as the vanguards of a technological revolution that transcends mere computation. At their core, AI and ML are the offspring of humanity's pursuit of creating machines that mimic cognitive functions and exhibit autonomous decision-making. Yet, their essence extends far beyond mere imitation, unfurling a captivating narrative that involves the convergence of multidisciplinary fields, intricate algorithms, and the boundless expanse of data.

AI: Beyond Human Replication

Artificial Intelligence is a multidimensional concept that encapsulates the creation of systems capable of performing tasks that typically require human intelligence. It stands as a testament to our audacious ambition to replicate, if not transcend, human cognitive abilities. AI is not confined to mere rule-based programming; instead, it traverses the terrain of machine perception, natural language understanding, problem-solving, and even emotional cognition. From virtual personal assistants that understand and respond to our commands, to the surreal marvels of self-driving cars that navigate through the labyrinth of roads, AI is redefining the fabric of our existence.

Machine Learning: Illuminating Patterns within Data

Within the vast cosmos of AI, Machine Learning emerges as a radiant star, characterized by its ability to empower systems with the capacity to learn from data. It dispenses with the need for explicit programming, allowing algorithms to iteratively learn from examples, adapt, and improve their performance over time. Machine Learning's scope spans a spectrum of paradigms, each unveiling a unique facet of its prowess:

Supervised Learning: The realm where algorithms are bestowed with labeled training data to predict or classify future outcomes. It's the compass guiding email spam filters to differentiate between the mundane and the malicious.

Unsupervised Learning: Here, algorithms explore data without predefined labels, uncovering hidden patterns and structures. It's the compass guiding data analysts in revealing market segments from customer behavior.

Reinforcement Learning: Like a digital embodiment of reward-based learning, algorithms navigate an environment, learning through trial, error, and feedback. It's the intelligence behind teaching a machine to play games, make financial decisions, and even control complex industrial processes.

The Intersection and Expanding Frontiers

The confluence of AI and ML forms an intricate tapestry where AI provides the overarching framework, while ML serves as its dynamic engine. The scope of this synergy extends from robotics and healthcare to finance and entertainment, birthing innovations that were once the realm of speculative fiction. The promise of AI and ML lies not just in accomplishing tasks but in augmenting human capabilities – amplifying our potential to decipher intricate data patterns, making informed decisions, and unearthing insights that elude human cognition.

As we traverse this awe-inspiring landscape, the quest to demystify intelligence and reshape the contours of possibility continues. The journey through the realms of AI and ML is a perpetual exploration, where the boundaries of human imagination converge with the algorithmic symphonies of machines, forever altering the way we perceive, interact with, and harness the power of technology.

B. Historical evolution and key milestones

The annals of technological evolution bear witness to an extraordinary saga – the birth, evolution, and maturation of Artificial Intelligence (AI) and Machine Learning (ML). From early philosophical ponderings to the electrifying strides of contemporary neural networks, this journey weaves together the threads of human curiosity, scientific endeavor, and the relentless pursuit of unlocking the secrets of cognition in machines.

Antecedents: Seeds of AI Sprout

The roots of AI can be traced back to antiquity, where myth and philosophy flirted with the notion of artificial beings. From the enchanting tales of Pygmalion sculpting his ivory beloved to medieval alchemical pursuits, echoes of our desire to breathe life into the inanimate resound across epochs. Yet, the seeds of modern AI were sown in the 20th century.

Dartmouth Workshop (1956): The AI Dawn

In a momentous gathering at Dartmouth College in 1956, the term "Artificial Intelligence" was coined, ushering in an era of scientific exploration. Visionaries like John McCarthy, Marvin Minsky, and Nathaniel Rochester laid the foundation for AI, with ambitions to create machines that could mimic human intelligence. This event marks the inception of AI as a formal academic discipline.

Early Successes and AI Winter (1950s - 1970s): The Rollercoaster Ride

The 1950s saw the birth of programs like the Logic Theorist, capable of proving mathematical theorems, and the General Problem Solver, a glimpse into problem-solving AI. However, the high expectations gave way to an "AI Winter" in the 1970s due to computational limitations and unrealized promises.

Expert Systems and the Second AI Spring (1980s - 1990s): Revival and Revolution

The AI torch was reignited with the development of expert systems that encoded human expertise into software.

Technologies like MYCIN, a medical diagnostic system, showcased the potential of AI in real-world applications. The 1990s marked the "Second AI Spring," as AI found renewed relevance with advancements in neural networks, robotics, and natural language processing.

Machine Learning Renaissance (2000s - 2010s): Pioneering Algorithms

The emergence of vast datasets and computational power propelled Machine Learning into the spotlight. Support Vector Machines, Random Forests, and Neural Networks resurged, propelling breakthroughs in image recognition, language translation, and game-playing prowess.

Deep Learning Revolution (2010s - Present): A Quantum Leap

The meteoric rise of Deep Learning, driven by Convolutional Neural Networks and Recurrent Neural Networks, birthed unprecedented achievements. AlphaGo's conquest of the ancient game, self-driving cars navigating complex terrains, and language models generating coherent text stand as hallmarks of this era.

Contemporary Landscape and Future Horizons

In the present day, AI and ML stand not as abstract concepts, but as integral components of our daily lives. Virtual assistants anticipate our needs, recommendation systems guide our choices, and autonomous vehicles redefine transportation. The future promises an integration of AI into healthcare, climate modeling, and even our quest for extraterrestrial intelligence.

The journey from philosophical musings to AI-driven reality is a testament to human perseverance and innovation. As we traverse the epochs, the tapestry of AI and ML unfolds, intertwining past achievements with present breakthroughs, weaving a narrative that underscores the boundless potential of human imagination and the infinite possibilities that await us on the technological frontier.

C. Interdisciplinary nature of AI and ML

In the grand theater of human intellectual pursuit, Artificial Intelligence (AI) and Machine Learning (ML) emerge as the maestros, orchestrating an interdisciplinary symphony that harmonizes the diverse strains of knowledge. Their allure lies not just in their computational elegance, but in their profound capacity to bridge the chasms between fields as varied as neuroscience, mathematics, psychology, and linguistics, uniting them in a captivating ballet of discovery and innovation.

From Neurons to Networks: The Brain-Machine Pas de Deux

At the heart of AI and ML's interdisciplinary dance lies an

intimate waltz with neuroscience. As we seek to replicate the intricacies of human cognition, insights from neural networks illuminate our path. The very architecture of artificial neural networks draws inspiration from the synaptic connections within our brains. Neurons, dendrites, and synapses become metaphors for layers, nodes, and weights, merging biology and computation into a harmonious whole.

Mathematics: The Prima Ballerina of AI

In this performance, mathematics takes center stage, guiding the intricate choreography of algorithms and models. Probability theory pirouettes gracefully, guiding the uncertainty of data. Linear algebra elegantly transforms and rotates data dimensions, while calculus orchestrates the art of optimization, allowing machines to learn and evolve. The enigmatic elegance of mathematics is the underpinning that breathes life into AI and ML, transforming abstract concepts into tangible results.

Language and Semantics: The Ballet of Communication

Language, the quintessential mark of human communication, is an integral partner in this dance. Natural Language Processing (NLP) endeavors to decode the semantic tapestry of human speech and text. Syntax and semantics tango to decipher context, sentiment, and meaning, unraveling the complexity of language through algorithms that blend linguistics with computation.

Perception and Sensation: The Dance of Vision and Sound

AI and ML extend their embrace to the realm of perception, encapsulating computer vision and audio analysis. These fields blur the lines between science and art as they seek to replicate human sight and hearing. Computer vision algorithms learn to perceive patterns in images, while audio analysis systems unravel the intricate melodies and harmonies of sound waves, transforming pixels and audio signals into comprehensible data.

Social Sciences and Ethics: A Dance of Reflection

Even the corridors of social sciences find their reflection in AI and ML. As we entrust algorithms to make decisions and predictions, ethical considerations come to the fore. The quest for unbiased, fair, and transparent models becomes a dance of introspection, where insights from philosophy, psychology, and sociology guide the steps towards responsible AI development.

Futuristic Pas de Deux: AI and ML in Unison

As this interdisciplinary ballet unfolds, its future takes center stage, promising a symphony of unimaginable harmony. The dance continues as AI and ML venture into personalized medicine, environmental conservation, and the frontiers of space exploration. The ensemble cast of disciplines, from biology to astronomy, converge to amplify our capabilities and unravel the mysteries of the universe.

In this grand performance, AI and ML emerge not just as technological marvels, but as ambassadors of collaboration, inviting diverse disciplines to join hands and dance together towards a future where innovation knows no boundaries. The interdisciplinary nature of AI and ML stands as a testament to human potential, celebrating the unison of knowledge, creativity, and curiosity in an awe-inspiring choreography that reshapes the very fabric of our world.

CHAPTER 2

Machine Learning Fundamentals

In the intricate labyrinth of the digital age, where data flows like a river of binary consciousness, Machine Learning emerges as the compass guiding us through the uncharted territories of information. With algorithms as our guides and data as our fuel, we embark on a transformative odyssey – a journey that transcends mere programming and delves into the realm of machines that learn, adapt, and evolve. The fundamentals of Machine Learning are the key to unlocking this remarkable transformation, unraveling the tapestry of algorithms, patterns, and insights that dance across the canvas of data, and shaping the very landscape of our technological future. So, tighten your intellectual harness, for we are about to embark on a voyage where the ordinary becomes extraordinary, and where the intersection of mathematics, statistics, and computer science paves the way to machines that not only compute but comprehend.

A. Types of machine learning: supervised, unsupervised, reinforcement learning

In the ethereal realm of Machine Learning, a trio of paradigms emerges, each casting its own unique spell upon the digital landscape. These paradigms, akin to facets of a multifaceted gem, are Supervised Learning, Unsupervised Learning, and Reinforcement Learning. They form the cornerstone of intelligent systems, a testament to the malleability of data and the ingenuity of human innovation.

Supervised Learning: Sculpting from Labeled Clay

Supervised Learning is the enchantress that thrives on guidance, fed by the delicate dance of labeled data. Picture it as an artist crafting a masterpiece guided by a mentor's brushstrokes. Here, algorithms are akin to proteges learning from a seasoned maestro. They ingest historical data, replete with inputs and corresponding outputs, and endeavor to learn the underlying patterns. Just as a painter extracts themes from past masterpieces, these algorithms uncover relationships between variables and create predictive models that can generate outputs for new inputs. The realm of classification and regression finds its muse here - whether it's discerning between spam and genuine emails or predicting stock prices with the grace of a clairvoyant.

Unsupervised Learning: The Alchemy of Hidden Patterns

Unsupervised Learning unfurls its enigmatic banner in the realm of the unknown, where data lacks the delicate brushstrokes of labels. It is akin to a treasure hunter venturing into uncharted territories, deciphering cryptic maps without a guiding compass. Algorithms here are the modern-day alchemists, distilling patterns from data through clustering and association. They discern groupings in customer behaviors, segmenting markets without predefined categories. They unearth associations, revealing that customers who buy bread are also more likely to buy butter. The symphony of this paradigm is a testament to the latent beauty buried within data, waiting to be unearthed.

Reinforcement Learning: The Symphony of Trial and Reward

Picture a relentless adventurer in an unfamiliar land, learning the lay of the land through trial, error, and the allure of rewards. That is the essence of Reinforcement Learning. Here, algorithms don the mantle of learners traversing a dynamic environment, making decisions and refining actions to maximize cumulative rewards. The synergy between actions and consequences is orchestrated by a feedback loop, fine-tuning strategies in response to outcomes. This is the backbone of autonomous systems, teaching machines to play games, control robots, and even optimize financial portfolios. The dance between exploration and exploitation in Reinforcement Learning is a reflection of human learning, an epitome of machines imitating our quest for mastery.

In the Tapestry of Intelligence: Unity in Diversity

The harmonious interplay of these paradigms paints a rich tapestry of intelligent systems. Each, with its distinct flavors and nuances, stitches together the fabric of AI's progress. Supervised

Learning, the mentor's guiding hand; Unsupervised Learning, the revealer of hidden gems; and Reinforcement Learning, the trailblazer of autonomous acumen. Together, they resonate the grandeur of human intellect, crafting algorithms that not only calculate but comprehend, algorithms that not only process data but perceive, algorithms that emulate the quintessence of our cognitive journey through the ever-evolving expanse of information.

B. Model representation and evaluation metrics

In the digital atelier of Machine Learning, the creation of a model is akin to sculpting an intricate masterpiece, while the choice of evaluation metrics becomes the lens through which its brilliance is discerned. This artistry, grounded in the realms of mathematics and statistics, breathes life into algorithms, transforming raw data into predictive insights. As we venture into this realm, we unravel the elegant dance of model representation and the symphony of evaluation metrics that guide us towards intelligence's doorstep.

Model Representation: Sculpting Algorithms with Finesse

Imagine the creation of a sculpture: a block of raw material hewn into a vision of artistry. Similarly, model representation is the delicate chiseling of algorithms from the raw bedrock of data. This process involves selecting an appropriate algorithm or architecture that aligns with the nature of the problem at hand. Just as a sculptor selects tools to match the medium, a data scientist crafts models – be it decision trees, support vector machines, or neural networks – to best capture the essence of the data's patterns.

But like a sculptor's meticulous attention to detail, parameters within models must be fine-tuned. Hyperparameters – the dials and knobs that govern a model's behavior – demand judicious adjustment. Much like the interplay of light and shadow defining a sculpture's contours, hyperparameters shape a model's performance. Tuning them is an art, requiring a blend of intuition and experimentation, with the ultimate goal of creating an algorithmic masterpiece that mirrors the intricacies of the real world.

Evaluation Metrics: The Lens of Perfection

As the sculptor steps back to appraise the sculpture, so too must data scientists wield the lens of evaluation metrics to gauge their models' fidelity. These metrics – the critical eye of the machine learning world – encompass a spectrum that measures precision, recall, accuracy, and F1 scores, echoing the sculptor's attention to proportion, balance, and form. Each metric offers a distinct perspective, allowing us to discern a model's strengths and weaknesses.

Consider accuracy, the most familiar of these metrics, as the artist's first impression – the overall impression of the sculpture.

Precision and recall, akin to the balance between fine detail and overall structure in sculpture, offer insights into a model's ability to classify correctly and capture relevant instances. F1 score harmonizes precision and recall into a single measure, akin to an art critic summarizing a sculpture's essence.

But, just as a sculpture's allure transcends mere measurement, the human element in machine learning cannot be overlooked. Human judgment, domain expertise, and the contextual nuances that metrics might not capture, play a pivotal role in the evaluation process. Just as the viewer's emotional connection enriches the perception of a sculpture, so too does a data scientist's intuition enhance the interpretation of metrics.

A Tapestry Woven in Code and Intuition

In the intersection of model representation and evaluation metrics, we witness the seamless melding of art and science. The code we write, the models we create, and the metrics we deploy become the brushstrokes of a digital masterpiece. Just as sculptors leave their mark on stone, data scientists etch their imprint on algorithms, invoking patterns hidden within data's embrace. And as a sculptor's creation stands illuminated by a critic's discerning eye, so too do machine learning models shine under the scrutiny of evaluation metrics, their performance illuminating the path toward intelligence's summit.

C. Bias-variance trade-off and overfitting

In the realm of Machine Learning, a delicate dance unfurls between the twin specters of Bias and Variance, a pas de deux that shapes the very essence of model performance. Alongside this intricate choreography emerges the enigmatic figure of Overfitting, a seductive waltz with data that can ensnare even the most sophisticated algorithms. As we step into this enthralling performance, we unravel the intertwined narratives of Bias-Variance Trade-off and Overfitting, two partners that weave a symphony of predictive power and potential pitfalls.

Bias-Variance Trade-off: The Ballet of Balance

Picture a tightrope walker, teetering between extremes – this is the Bias-Variance Trade-off. On one hand, Bias represents a model's simplification, akin to viewing a complex landscape through a single lens. A high-bias model might miss intricate patterns, like a sketch artist glossing over details. On the other hand, Variance epitomizes the model's sensitivity, where the slightest gust of noise or irregularity disrupts equilibrium. A high-variance model captures every nuance, including the noise – akin to a painter faithfully depicting every grain of sand, but losing sight of the whole picture.

Achieving the ideal balance is like orchestrating a delicate ballet – a model must embrace Bias to capture general trends, yet embrace Variance to adapt to the intricacies within. Just as a choreographer guides dancers to synchronize their movements, a data scientist adjusts the bias-variance equilibrium through techniques like regularization or selecting appropriate model complexity. This dance, this finely tuned ballet of compromise, creates models that generalize well to unseen data, wielding predictive prowess without succumbing to the siren call of overfitting.

Overfitting: The Seductive Tango of Complexity

Enter Overfitting, the charmer who entices models into an intricate tango with their training data. Much like a partner who becomes lost in the dance, an overfit model becomes enamored with the idiosyncrasies of the training set, mirroring even the quirks and noise. Just as an artist smitten by intricate details might overlook the grand canvas, an overfit model might falter when presented with new, unseen data – stumbling in a dance it has not rehearsed.

This seductive tango is deceptive. It showcases flawless steps within the familiar, yet crumbles upon encountering the unknown. Data scientists must play the role of vigilant choreographers, ensuring the model's performance transcends mere memorization and instead embraces the essence of the data's true form. Techniques like cross-validation and early stopping emerge as the choreographer's baton, guiding the dance of model training with a discerning eye.

Harmony in Complexity: Crafting Intelligence

In this symphony of complexity and balance, Bias-Variance Trade-off and Overfitting create a harmonious duet, each influencing the other's cadence. As an orchestra achieves synchrony, so too must models navigate this intricate interplay. A model that embodies Bias-Variance equilibrium, shunning the siren call of overfitting, becomes a masterpiece of predictive prowess – capable of interpreting new melodies, capturing the essence of data's composition, and choreographing elegant predictions with every step.

The world of Machine Learning beckons us to master this ballet, to become conductors of complexity, and choreographers of balance. Just as a ballet reaches crescendo through every twirl and leap, so too does the intelligence of our models elevate as we harmonize the dance of Bias-Variance Trade-off and prudently navigate the seductive embrace of Overfitting.

CHAPTER 3

Data Preprocessing and Feature Engineering

In the grand atelier of Machine Learning, where algorithms forge the path to digital cognition, lies a transformative process akin to sculpting raw material into refined artistry. This process, known as Data Preprocessing and Feature Engineering, is the alchemical fusion of creativity and precision, turning the rough stones of data into polished gems of insight. Just as a master sculptor shapes clay into timeless forms, data scientists mold and refine information, transcending noise and imperfections to unveil the hidden beauty beneath. This symphony of preparation and refinement sets the stage for models to dance with elegance and predict the future with grace.

A. Data cleaning and transformation techniques

In the ethereal realm of Machine Learning, where algorithms unfurl the tapestry of intelligence, lies a pivotal act of sorcery – the art of Data Cleaning and Transformation. This enchanting process, akin to alchemy, transmutes the raw ore of data into a gleaming treasure trove of insights. Just as ancient alchemists sought to turn base metals into gold, data scientists wield their craft to distill raw data into a pure elixir of knowledge. This journey, filled with incantations of missing values, anomalies, and skewed distributions, weaves a tale of turning chaos into order and unraveling truth from the cacophony of noise.

Data Cleaning: A Journey to Purity

Imagine a skilled jeweler, meticulously chipping away impurities from a precious gemstone. This is the essence of data cleaning – the process of meticulously removing anomalies, inconsistencies, and errors from the dataset. Missing values, those enigmatic gaps in the mosaic of information, are woven together with imputation techniques, restoring completeness to the picture. Outliers, those rebellious notes that disrupt the symphony, are either tamed or given voice, depending on their significance to the narrative. The noise, like a discordant echo, is silenced, allowing the true melody of the data to resonate.

Data Transformation: The Alchemical Metamorphosis

Just as alchemists sought to transform the mundane into the extraordinary, data transformation techniques conjure magic upon the dataset. The transformation is an intricate ballet of scaling, centering, and warping – each step refining the data's characteristics. Feature scaling, a symphony of normalization and standardization, harmonizes disparate variables, ensuring no individual note overshadows the melody. Principal Component Analysis (PCA), reminiscent of an artist's palette, combines colors to capture the essence of the painting in fewer strokes. Logarithmic and power transformations, like a sorcerer's spell, unravel skewed distributions, making them ready for the dance of algorithms.

Dimensionality Reduction: The Art of Elegance

In the grand gallery of data, dimensionality reduction emerges as a masterstroke – a way to condense intricate information without compromising essence. Much like an artist using minimalist strokes to convey depth, techniques like PCA and t-SNE distill high-dimensional data into elegant representations. This process uncovers latent patterns, exposes hidden relationships, and empowers models to discern the signal amidst the noise.

Harmony Amid Complexity: Crafting Intelligence

In this mystical dance of Data Cleaning and Transformation, the true alchemy lies in striking the balance between preservation and refinement. The aim is not to alter the data's essence, but to unveil its true brilliance. As the data scientist navigates through missing values and reshapes distributions, they channel the essence of both archaeologist and artist, resurrecting truth and crafting insights.

This journey from raw data to refined truth is an intricate symphony, a saga of purification and metamorphosis. Just as alchemists turned base elements into gold, so do data scientists convert raw data into the gold of knowledge, unveiling truths that were previously hidden in the shadows. The transformative power of Data Cleaning and Transformation is a testament to human ingenuity, breathing life into data and forging a path towards the pinnacle of intelligent discovery.

B. Feature selection and extraction methods

In the grand symphony of Machine Learning, where algorithms compose melodies of intelligence, a duet of techniques emerges – Feature Selection and Feature Extraction. These virtuosos wield their batons to craft a harmonious arrangement from the cacophony of data, curating a masterful composition that captivates models and resonates with predictive power. Imagine a maestro conducting an orchestra; each instrument, carefully chosen and skillfully played, contributes to the grand opus. Similarly, feature selection and extraction techniques shape the ensemble of variables, optimizing performance and unveiling the true essence of the data's melody.

Feature Selection: The Composer's Elegance

Much like a composer meticulously selects and arranges musical notes, feature selection sculpts a dataset, retaining only the most melodious variables. This is not a mere pruning of excess, but an artful curation, guided by the principle that less can indeed be more. Just as a symphony might lose its charm if every instrument played at once, a model can suffer from the curse of the Curse of Dimensionality if bombarded with excessive variables.

Feature selection is the conductor's baton, elegantly weaving through the sea of variables, identifying those that contribute most to the predictive prowess of the model. The process can be as delicate as a pianist's touch – with techniques like Recursive Feature Elimination (RFE) peeling away layers of less influential features, or as intuitive as a conductor's intuition – guided by domain expertise and understanding of the data's context.

Feature Extraction: The Maestro of Transformation

Feature extraction, on the other hand, transforms the orchestration altogether, akin to a maestro interpreting a classic symphony in a new, innovative way. This technique derives new features from the original set, distilling complex information into a concise yet expressive form. Principal Component Analysis (PCA), for instance, is the virtuoso who conducts this transformation, condensing the data's richness into a compact representation while preserving its essence. Much like a conductor capturing the spirit of a timeless composition, feature extraction captures the essence of data, representing it in a manner that resonates deeply with models.

Harmony Amidst Complexity: Crafting Intelligence

In this symphony of Feature Selection and Extraction, the conductor's prowess lies in striking the balance between dimensionality reduction and information retention. The goal is not to merely compress the data, but to distill it into a form that captures its core essence – much like a conductor extracting the essence of a musical piece without losing its soul.

Just as a composer's pen creates a symphony, and a conductor's baton brings it to life, so do feature selection and extraction methods orchestrate the data, molding it into a harmonious ensemble that guides machine learning models towards profound insights. This journey from raw variables to refined melodies is an intricate masterpiece, an ode to the power of transformation, and a testament to the ability of human innovation to shape and elevate the realm of intelligence.

C. Handling missing data and outliers

In the vast ocean of data, where insights lie hidden beneath the waves, two formidable challenges emerge like tempestuous currents – Handling Missing Data and Confronting Outliers. These twin forces, while often disruptive, unveil themselves as vital markers on the journey towards meaningful analysis and accurate modeling. Just as seasoned sailors navigate treacherous waters, data scientists employ ingenious techniques to tame missing data and confront outliers, steering the ship of analysis towards the shores of knowledge.

Handling Missing Data: Stitching the Fabric of Knowledge

Imagine a map where certain regions remain uncharted – this is the world of missing data. These gaps, like unsolved puzzles, threaten to skew analysis and distort conclusions. Yet, within these gaps lie opportunities for enlightenment. Data scientists become modern-day cartographers, employing strategies to fill the voids while preserving the data's integrity.

Imputation, a technique reminiscent of ancient mariners plotting their course, is the art of estimating missing values based on observed data. It's a delicate balance, much like completing a partial painting while ensuring the hues remain consistent. Statistical methods, from mean and median imputation to more advanced algorithms, weave threads of estimated values, completing the fabric of knowledge.

However, the journey is not without its challenges. Data scientists must tread cautiously, mindful of potential biases and distortions that imputation might introduce. Just as mariners seek to avoid treacherous reefs, these navigators of data must safeguard against pitfalls that lurk in the currents of imputed values.

Confronting Outliers: Unveiling the Extraordinary

Outliers, those daring anomalies that disrupt the rhythm of data, evoke both skepticism and fascination. Much like eccentric explorers who push the boundaries of known territories, outliers offer a window into unique phenomena, untapped insights, or data collection errors. Confronting them requires a blend of vigilance and discernment.

Robust techniques, akin to navigating turbulent waves, equip data scientists to discern genuine outliers from noisy fluctuations. Z-score and modified Z-score tests, like compasses pointing true north, identify values that diverge significantly from the norm. Box plots, reminiscent of seafarers' charts, provide a visual guide to the distribution of data, spotlighting potential anomalies.

Yet, not all outliers are castaways. Just as explorers might bring back exotic treasures, some outliers carry valuable insights. Domain knowledge, like a seasoned explorer's compass, helps distinguish between valuable discoveries and mere distractions. Data scientists tread the line between filtering out noise and preserving the extraordinary, much like sailors discerning between hidden treasures and mirages on distant shores.

Crafting a Narrative Amidst Chaos: Illuminating Truths

In the dance between missing data and outliers, a story emerges – one of diligent exploration and artful interpretation. Data scientists, like skilled navigators, choose their tools wisely, steering their analyses towards clarity amidst the chaos. Imputation and outlier handling, while demanding, contribute to a coherent narrative that unfurls the truths lying beneath the surface.

Just as mariners chart their course, data scientists sail through the sea of data, navigating the complexities of missing values and outliers. Through their expertise, they transform these challenges into guiding stars, illuminating the path towards informed decision-making and unveiling insights that shimmer like hidden treasures beneath the waves.

Part II

Machine Learning Algorithms and Techniques

CHAPTER 4

Linear and Logistic Regression

In the grand theater of data analysis, where variables converse in a symphony of patterns and predictions, Linear and Logistic Regression emerge as the virtuosos – the maestros who unravel the intricate melodies of relationships. Imagine a storyteller who weaves the threads of cause and effect, transforming data points into narrative arcs. Linear Regression, with its elegant lines, unveils the secrets of continuous numerical connections, while Logistic Regression, like a cunning detective, deciphers the mysteries of binary outcomes. As we delve into this mesmerizing duet, prepare to embark on a journey where data speaks, and algorithms listen – where insights spring forth like poetry from the artistry of regression analysis.

A. Principles and applications of linear regression

In the symphony of data analysis, where patterns whisper and correlations murmur, Linear Regression emerges as the conductor, orchestrating the harmonious dance of variables. Like a philosophical sage, it seeks to uncover the profound connections between numerical entities, transforming raw data into predictive insights. As we embark on this intellectual odyssey, prepare to traverse the principles and applications of Linear Regression – a journey that bridges theory and practice, unveiling the magic of turning numbers into knowledge.

Principles: The Elegance of Linearity

At its core, Linear Regression embodies the elegant principle of linearity, akin to a master painter using straight strokes to create depth and form. It postulates that relationships between variables can be approximated by a straight line, where one variable serves as the predictor, while the other acts as the response. This mathematical elegance extends beyond the canvas of art, resonating with real-world phenomena, from predicting housing prices based on square footage to estimating sales based on advertising expenditure.

The essence of Linear Regression lies in the quest to find the optimal line – one that minimizes the difference between predicted and actual values, much like an artist searching for the perfect brushstroke to capture the essence of a scene. The slope of this line embodies the relationship's strength, while the intercept anchors it to reality. It is a process of introspection and calculation, where statistics and intuition meld to shape a predictive masterpiece.

Applications: Unveiling Patterns, Guiding Decisions

Linear Regression's applications span a panoramic spectrum, from economics to medicine, illuminating relationships and informing decisions. In the realm of economics, it navigates the currents of supply and demand, guiding businesses in optimizing prices and quantities. In medicine, it serves as a diagnostic tool, predicting disease outcomes based on patient characteristics. Like a versatile actor donning different roles, Linear Regression adapts to various scenarios, unearthing insights that guide strategies, policies, and interventions.

In marketing, it becomes the oracle that deciphers customer behavior, enabling tailored campaigns and personalized recommendations. It transforms stock market data into forecasting tools, offering glimpses into financial futures. Environmental scientists wield it to analyze climate data, unraveling the threads of global trends. In each application, Linear Regression transforms data into wisdom, empowering stakeholders with predictive foresight and shaping the contours of decision-making landscapes.

The Tapestry of Intelligence: Insights Woven Through Linear Regression

In the realm of data alchemy, Linear Regression emerges as a potent elixir, transmuting raw data into actionable insights. Its principles resonate with the elegance of simplicity, while its applications span a tapestry of domains, from the intricacies of finance to the nuances of human health. Like an artist with a palette of equations, Linear Regression weaves patterns and relationships, guiding us through the labyrinth of data, and illuminating the path towards informed choices. As we delve deeper, we uncover not just a technique, but a profound manifestation of intelligence – a bridge that connects the empirical realm with the ethereal world of predictions, where data speaks in a language understood by those who seek to unravel its secrets.

B. Logistic regression for classification problems

In the grand saga of data analysis, where questions demand answers and decisions yearn for clarity, Logistic Regression emerges as the sentinel of classification, a binary oracle that discerns the intricate boundary between two worlds. Imagine a wise sage who reads the patterns of data, foreseeing outcomes as probabilities dance in the ethereal space between zero and one. As we embark on this intellectual odyssey, prepare to immerse yourself in the depths of Logistic Regression – a journey that demystifies the principles, showcases the applications, and unveils the artistry of transforming data into decisions.

Principles: Probability's Eloquent Messenger

At its essence, Logistic Regression is the messenger of probability, the interpreter of binary outcomes. It adheres to the principles of classic Linear Regression, but its canvas is a realm where only two hues exist – 0 and 1, yes or no, success or failure. Like an architect plotting a threshold, it crafts a decision boundary that separates the two classes, encapsulating the essence of a classification problem.

The magic of Logistic Regression lies in its transformation, as it employs a sigmoid function to translate linear combinations into probabilities. This function, akin to a conductor moderating the symphony, gracefully curves data points towards the realms of possibility. The result? Predictions that reside in the domain of certainty and uncertainty, striking a balance between conviction and ambiguity.

Applications: From Diagnostics to Finance, the Classifying Alchemy

Logistic Regression's applications span a panorama of domains, from medical diagnostics to credit scoring, unraveling the tapestry of binary challenges. In medicine, it becomes the oracle that predicts disease outcomes, assessing the probability of a diagnosis based on patient characteristics. Like a forensic investigator, it deciphers fraud detection in financial transactions, identifying anomalies and safeguarding assets. Marketing campaigns find their guiding star in Logistic Regression, aligning efforts with the probability of customer responses.

In sentiment analysis, it navigates the sea of text, discerning positive from negative sentiment with uncanny accuracy. In quality control, it serves as a sentinel, classifying products as faulty or flawless based on measurable attributes. Across these diverse scenarios, Logistic Regression shines as a beacon, transforming data into decision-making tools, and equipping stakeholders with predictive insights that illuminate the path forward.

The Binary Enigma: A Symphony of Knowledge

In the realm of data's mysteries, Logistic Regression stands as an enigma, unraveling the binary code that underpins classification problems. Its principles, steeped in probability, resonate with the certainty and uncertainty that define binary outcomes. Its applications, like an artisan's touch, refine decision-making processes across domains, from healthcare to finance, from marketing to quality control.

Logistic Regression is more than an algorithm; it is a symphony of knowledge that elevates data to decision, uncertainty to insight. It is the embodiment of data's binary soul, capturing the essence of the yes-no dichotomy and transforming it into a landscape of probabilities. As we delve deeper, we uncover not just a tool, but a profound manifestation of classification intelligence – a bridge that connects the abstract realm of data to the tangible realm of informed choices, where data whispers its secrets to those who seek to understand its dual nature.

C. Regularization techniques: L1, L2, Elastic Net

In the realm of predictive modeling, where data's tapestry weaves intricate patterns, Regularization techniques emerge as virtuosos wielding an artist's brush – their strokes shaping the very essence of algorithms. Enter the stage L1, L2, and the harmonious composition of Elastic Net, each a maestro orchestrating the delicate balance between complexity and overfitting. As we unravel this symphony of sculpting precision, prepare to embark on a journey through the enchanting world of Regularization – a journey that marries mathematical finesse with predictive prowess.

L1 Regularization: The Oracle of Sparsity

Imagine an architect purging the superfluous to reveal a masterpiece – this is the role of L1 Regularization, also known as Lasso. It is the alchemical process that transforms an algorithm's intricate melody into a sparse symphony. Lasso's magic lies in its ability to simultaneously minimize the sum of squared errors and impose a constraint on the absolute values of coefficients. This constraint, akin to an art curator's discerning eye, sculpts a model that prunes irrelevant features, leaving only the most impactful variables to sing their harmonious tune.

L1 Regularization's elegance is in its parsimony. It selects and discards with finesse, like an author editing a story to its essence.

Its impact reverberates across domains, from genetics to finance, where feature selection and interpretability are paramount. Just as an artist wields a scalpel with precision, L1 Regularization uncovers the hidden gems within data, crafting models that gracefully balance simplicity and predictive power.

L2 Regularization: The Architect of Equilibrium

In the cathedral of algorithms, L2 Regularization, or Ridge, emerges as the architect of equilibrium. It tempers the exuberance of complex models, gently guiding them towards stability. Picture a gardener meticulously tending to a bonsai tree – this is Ridge's role in the world of data. It tames wild coefficients by adding a penalty term that squares their values, nudging them towards moderation without banishing them entirely.

Ridge's impact is transformative, like a master craftsman balancing form and function. It reduces multicollinearity, quelling the discordant echoes of correlated features. Ridge shines in scenarios where multicollinearity reigns, from economics to engineering, untangling the threads of influence. Just as an architect harmonizes design elements, L2 Regularization orchestrates a model that embraces complexity while curbing excesses, ensuring harmony between predictive performance and stability.

Elastic Net: The Maestro of Harmonious Blends

Enter Elastic Net, the polymath that harmonizes L1 and L2 Regularization in a symphony of proportion. Like an artist mixing colors to create a balanced palette, Elastic Net blends the sparsity-seeking L1 with the equilibrium-seeking L2. It inherits the strengths of its predecessors while mitigating their weaknesses, striking a delicate balance between feature selection and coefficient shrinkage.

Elastic Net's allure lies in its adaptability, its power to navigate the subtleties of data. It thrives in scenarios where high-dimensional data meets multicollinearity, like an interpreter deciphering a multilingual text. From genomics to social sciences, Elastic Net crafts a model that resonates with precision and resilience, capturing the nuances of data's language while mitigating the cacophony of noise.

The Symphony of Precision: A Harmonious Ensemble

In the tapestry of predictive modeling, Regularization techniques – L1, L2, and Elastic Net – compose a symphony that transcends mere algorithms. L1's sparsity, L2's equilibrium, and Elastic Net's fusion encapsulate the art of sculpting precision. They harmonize complexity with simplicity, distilling the essence of data's narrative into models that sing with predictive prowess.

Regularization, like an artisan's touch, transforms models into masterpieces – sparse yet impactful, complex yet stable, harmonious yet precise. It is the fusion of mathematical ingenuity and predictive artistry, a testament to the alchemical power of data analysis. As we journey through Regularization's rhapsody, we witness the culmination of elegance and efficacy, a crescendo that elevates algorithms to symphonies of insight.

CHAPTER 5

Decision Trees and Random Forests

Amidst the data-rich landscape where insights lie hidden like gems beneath the earth, Decision Trees and Random Forests emerge as the guardians of clarity and predictive might. Envision a verdant forest where each tree represents a story waiting to be told, a decision ready to be made. Here, the symphony of data orchestrates the growth of branches, leading to conclusions, while Random Forests, like a council of wise sages, harmonize these individual stories into a collective narrative. As we venture into this arboreal realm of intelligence, prepare to be captivated by the elegance and power of Decision Trees and the enchanting tapestry woven by their assembly into Random Forests.

A. Decision tree construction and traversal

In the labyrinth of data's intricacies, where patterns beckon and insights remain concealed, Decision Tree construction and traversal emerge as the torchbearers of clarity and revelation. Imagine a master cartographer mapping uncharted territories – this is the role of Decision Trees, charting the course of data's narrative through a series of choices. Traversal, akin to an explorer's journey, follows these pathways, unveiling the story etched

41

within. As we embark on this intellectual voyage, prepare to unravel the mysteries of Decision Tree construction and the intrepid traversal that navigates their branches – a journey that marries algorithmic precision with the art of decoding data's secrets.

Decision Tree Construction: The Elegance of Choice

At its core, Decision Tree construction embodies the elegance of choice, a process akin to a chess grandmaster calculating every move. It unravels the web of data, iteratively selecting features that best divide the dataset, much like a cartographer drawing lines to demarcate territories. Each division, known as a split, is a strategic maneuver that maximizes information gain, revealing the most crucial details.

Entropy and Gini Impurity, the architects of choice, measure the impurity of a node's class distribution – guiding Decision Trees to select splits that enhance purity and classification power. Like an artist seeking balance in a painting's composition, Decision Tree construction seeks equilibrium between exploration and exploitation, between granularity and generalization.

Traversal: Journey through the Foliage

Once constructed, the Decision Tree stands as a map, ready to guide explorers through its foliage of choices. Traversal, the process of navigation, follows the trails of splits and nodes, revealing a story written in binary decisions. Imagine an explorer delving into the heart of a dense forest, following the path that beckons – this is the role of traversal, where each split leads to new insights, each node whispers a piece of the narrative.

Traversal is more than a sequence of steps; it's an excavation of knowledge. It embraces the spirit of exploration, delving deeper into the branches to uncover the truth. Whether through depth-first or breadth-first traversal, the explorer's torch unveils not just the route but the rationale, as each split paints a vivid stroke in the canvas of understanding.

The Map and the Journey: Envoys of Intelligence

In the realm of data's enigmas, Decision Tree construction and traversal stand as envoys of intelligence, translating the language of variables into a narrative of insights. Their principles embody the elegance of choice, the quest for purity, and the journey of exploration. Together, they craft a symphony of decision-making, where data's whispers evolve into categorical verdicts.

The journey through Decision Tree traversal is an adventure, an odyssey through the realms of splits and nodes. It is the unraveling of data's secrets, the unwrapping of choices made by algorithms. The combination of construction and traversal is more than an algorithmic process; it is an art that empowers data scientists to transform complexity into clarity, and transform data into decisions. As we delve deeper, we witness not just an analysis, but a profound manifestation of intelligence – a bridge that connects the empirical domain with the realm of actionable insights, where algorithms whisper their truths to those who listen.

B. Ensemble learning and random forest algorithm

In the realm of predictive modeling, where accuracy is the beacon and noise the labyrinth, Ensemble Learning emerges as the maestro, conducting a harmonious symphony that transcends the limitations of individual algorithms. At the heart of this symphony stands the virtuoso known as Random Forest – an algorithmic masterpiece that blends the wisdom of Decision Trees with the elegance of diversity. Picture a council of experts, each offering their insights, weaving a tapestry of predictions that resonates with unparalleled precision and resilience. As we delve into the artistry of Ensemble Learning and the orchestration of the Random Forest algorithm, prepare to be enthralled by the fusion of algorithms, the prowess of prediction, and the brilliance of collective intelligence.

Ensemble Learning: The Chorus of Diversity

Imagine a gathering of virtuoso musicians, each with a distinct instrument, coming together to create a harmonious symphony. This is the essence of Ensemble Learning – a paradigm that combines the strengths of multiple algorithms to forge a united predictive force. Just as diversity of perspective enriches decision-making, Ensemble Learning amalgamates a chorus of models, each offering its unique lens to the predictive narrative.

Ensemble methods, whether Bagging, Boosting, or Stacking, celebrate the wisdom of the crowd. They harmonize the strengths of various algorithms, compensating for individual weaknesses and biases. Just as a jury deliberates to reach a verdict, Ensemble Learning blends predictions to reach a consensus – a collective wisdom that often outshines the brilliance of its constituents.

Random Forest: The Arboreal Architects of Intelligence

At the heart of Ensemble Learning stands the magnum opus – the Random Forest algorithm. Imagine a lush forest, each tree representing an oracle with insights to share. Random Forest constructs an assembly of Decision Trees, each grown with a bootstrapped sample of data and making decisions based on a random subset of features. This diversification ensures that each tree is a distinct perspective, a unique expert in the council.

Random Forest's power lies in its ability to reduce overfitting and enhance predictive accuracy. By allowing each tree to cast its vote, the forest safeguards against the idiosyncrasies of individual models. It's akin to assembling a council of sages, each specialized in a different facet of knowledge, contributing to a collective intelligence that stands unrivaled.

The Symphony of Precision: A Multifaceted Masterpiece

Ensemble Learning and the Random Forest algorithm compose a symphony of intelligence that resounds with precision. Like a symphony conductor weaving melodies into harmonies, they orchestrate the individual notes of algorithms into a unified prediction that reverberates with clarity.

Random Forest's arboreal architects, guided by Ensemble Learning's principles, create a majestic forest where each tree contributes to the narrative. They stand as sentinels against overfitting, ensuring predictive prowess without succumbing to the noise. Together, they illuminate the path through data's labyrinth, transforming the chaos of information into a chorus of insights.

As we traverse the landscape of Ensemble Learning and the realm of Random Forests, we are witnesses to a multifaceted masterpiece – a symphony of algorithms that elevates predictive precision to new heights. In their union, we find not just an analysis, but an ode to the power of collective intelligence, where algorithms harmonize their voices to create a predictive symphony that resonates with the brilliance of human ingenuity.

C. Feature importance and interpretation

In the kingdom of data analysis, where variables hold the keys to hidden truths and predictive power, Feature Importance emerges as the torchbearer, casting its light on the enigmatic dance of features. Picture a detective's magnifying glass, revealing the significance of each clue in the intricate puzzle of data. Interpreting these insights, like a linguist decoding a cryptic script, transforms Feature Importance into a narrative that unveils the secrets within. As we embark on this intellectual odyssey, prepare to unravel the layers of significance and the delicate art of interpretation – a journey that bridges the gap between algorithmic precision and the human quest for understanding.

Feature Importance: The Elixir of Relevance

Imagine a grand ballroom, where each feature dances to its own rhythm, weaving a complex tale of interactions. Feature Importance strides onto the floor, bestowing each feature with a score that reflects its contribution to the predictive waltz. This score, much like a spotlight on the stage, guides data scientists towards the most influential players in the performance.

The methods for calculating Feature Importance vary – from the straightforward Gini Impurity in Decision Trees to the gradient-based insights of Gradient Boosting. Each algorithmic virtuoso bestows a unique lens through which to view the significance of features. As these scores emerge, features that orchestrate the symphony of prediction are spotlighted, while the quieter performers recede into the shadows.

Interpretation: The Dance of Insight

While Feature Importance marks the brightest stars on data's stage, interpretation is the dance that weaves these stars into a coherent narrative. Imagine an archaeologist piecing together fragments of an ancient artifact, unraveling a story etched in time. Interpretation is this delicate craft, a blend of domain expertise, intuition, and algorithmic guidance.

Interpreting Feature Importance requires context, much like a translator weaving words into a meaningful dialogue. Domain knowledge breathes life into the numbers, transforming scores into insights that guide decisions. The narrative unfolds as features reveal their roles in the broader context – are they influencers in financial forecasting, catalysts in medical diagnosis, or drivers of consumer behavior?

Crafting Insights: The Symphony of Understanding

The amalgamation of Feature Importance and interpretation is more than a sum of parts; it is a symphony that resonates with understanding. Feature Importance is the instrumental score, highlighting the melody within data's cacophony. Interpretation is the conductor's art, infusing meaning into the notes and harmonizing them into a coherent tune.

Through this symphony, data scientists embark on a journey of discovery – uncovering the relevance of features, grasping their implications, and shaping informed decisions. It is a journey that mirrors the process of artistic interpretation, transforming raw data into an insightful narrative that illuminates the path forward.

From Relevance to Revelation: The Alchemy of Insight

Feature Importance and interpretation are the alchemical catalysts that transform data's chaos into actionable insight. They stand as torchbearers in the realm of analysis, guiding data scientists through the maze of features towards the treasures of predictive power. As we delve into their world, we transcend mere numbers, unveiling the alchemy that converts data into wisdom – a testament to the fusion of mathematical precision and human intuition, where algorithms whisper their secrets, and we, the interpreters, listen with the ears of understanding.

CHAPTER 6

Support Vector Machines

In the theater of data analysis, where the curtain rises on complex patterns and classification conundrums, Support Vector Machines emerge as the virtuosos – the performers who paint the boundaries of decisions with a brush of mathematical elegance. Picture a tightrope walker gracefully traversing between realms of possibilities – this is the essence of Support Vector Machines, straddling the fine line between data points to create precise classifications. As we step into this world of decision beyond boundaries, prepare to be captivated by the unique cadence of Support Vector Machines – a symphony that harmonizes algorithmic sophistication with the art of discernment.

A. Geometric intuition of SVMs

Amidst the geometric tapestry of data, where dimensions intertwine and patterns ripple, Support Vector Machines (SVMs) emerge as the architects of distinction, sculpting decision boundaries with the precision of an artisan's chisel. Imagine a master sculptor transforming a block of marble into a masterpiece – this is the essence of SVMs, carving space into regions of classification. As we venture into the realm of SVMs, prepare to unravel the intricate geometric intuition that underpins their elegance – a journey that unveils the art of classification through the prism of space and geometry.

Space as Canvas: The Dimensional Landscape

Envision data as stars scattered across a celestial canvas, each point representing a unique entity. SVMs embark on a celestial mission, endeavoring to draw the clearest line between different categories. This line, known as the hyperplane, transforms the data's multidimensional universe into a two-dimensional realm where distinctions are etched.

The choice of hyperplane is not arbitrary; it is the sculptor's brushstroke that captures the essence of separation. SVMs seek the hyperplane with maximal margin – the widest gap between the classes. Like a tightrope walker's equilibrium, this margin provides the space for confident classification, minimizing the risk of missteps.

Support Vectors: The Pillars of Insight

In the artistic construction of SVMs, certain data points rise to prominence as the "support vectors." These points, much like the keystones in an architectural marvel, hold the hyperplane in place and define its orientation. They are the foundations of insight, dictating the structure of classification.

Imagine pulling a string taut through the support vectors – this string, the decision boundary, neatly bisects the data's landscape. The distance between the support vectors and the hyperplane, known as the margin, is maximized, forging a boundary of confident separation. SVMs, with their geometric finesse, ensure that no other hyperplane could cleave the classes with a larger gap.

Beyond Linear Boundaries: Kernel Magic

The artistic prowess of SVMs extends beyond linear boundaries. Just as a sculptor might shape clay into myriad forms, SVMs employ kernel functions to morph the data's space, projecting it into a higher dimension where linear separation becomes possible. This is the kernel magic, where linear boundaries in transformed dimensions can metamorphose into complex, nonlinear boundaries in the original space.

Imagine a magician's wand conjuring new dimensions – this is the role of kernels in SVMs. They bring forth a realm where intricate patterns become apparent, illuminating the data's hidden nuances. The artist's hand that once chiseled straight lines now crafts curves, spirals, and intricate forms, revealing the underlying structure that was once concealed.

Sculptors of Intelligence: SVMs as Artistry

In the symphony of algorithms, Support Vector Machines stand as sculptors of intelligence, transforming raw data into discerning decisions. Their geometric intuition weaves a narrative of separation, where the hyperplane becomes the stage for classification, the support vectors the pillars of insight, and kernels the brushes of transformation.

As we delve into the geometric intuition of SVMs, we witness not just an algorithm, but an artistic manifestation of classification. It is the fusion of geometry and intelligence, where the sculptor's precision meets the analyst's discernment. SVMs elevate data analysis to the realm of artistic interpretation, revealing patterns that dance across dimensions and carving out decision boundaries with the elegance of mathematical mastery.

B. Linear and non-linear kernel functions

In the realm of data analysis, where patterns and relationships weave intricate tales, Kernel Functions emerge as the maestros of transformation – composers of symphonies that elevate data from mere points to harmonious landscapes. Imagine a wizard's wand, conjuring dimensions and bending space to reveal hidden truths – this is the essence of Kernel Functions. As we step into the enchanting world of kernels, prepare to be captivated by their dual facets – the disciplined grace of Linear Kernels and the captivating allure of Non-linear Kernels – a journey that unfurls the magic of data transformation in its purest form.

Linear Kernels: The Elegance of Straightforward Harmony

Picture a perfectly choreographed dance, where partners move in synchrony with seamless grace. Linear Kernels orchestrate a similar ballet, where data points twirl and spin along straight paths of transformation. Like a symphony's conductor harmonizing the notes, Linear Kernels amplify existing dimensions, stretching or compressing them to create symmetry and balance.

The Linear Kernel is the mathematician's canvas of simplicity – a reflection of the original data, yet subtly nuanced. Imagine a mirror that faithfully replicates while subtly refining the image. Linear Kernels excel when relationships are straightforward, when data's song is a melody that flows with elegance along a linear path.

Non-linear Kernels: The Artistry of Dimensional Alchemy

Now, imagine a painter's palette, vibrant with colors that defy convention, blending and merging to create masterpieces that evoke emotions. Non-linear Kernels, much like these hues, infuse data with richness and complexity, transforming it into a multidimensional tapestry. They beckon data to dance through dimensions unknown, revealing patterns that lie hidden beneath the surface.

Gaussian, Polynomial, and Sigmoid Kernels are the brushes of this artistic transformation. They mold data into intricate forms, curving and folding space to illuminate patterns that defy linear simplicity. Non-linear Kernels shine when data's melody is intricate, when its rhythm is syncopated and woven into a symphony of complexities.

The Fusion: Harmony in Diversity

The brilliance of Kernel Functions lies not just in their individual virtuosity, but in their synergy. Linear Kernels lay the foundation, enhancing linear relationships and nurturing straightforward patterns. Non-linear Kernels, in turn, sweep across this foundation, breathing life into data's deeper intricacies and illuminating non-linear associations.

Imagine a duet between a pianist and a violinist – the piano's linear notes setting the stage for the violin's intricate melodies. Together, they create a harmonious ensemble that resonates with depth and richness. Linear and non-linear Kernel Functions form a similar duet, a fusion that marries simplicity and complexity, yielding a symphony of insights that captures data's true essence.

A Symphony of Transformation: Kernels as Virtuosos

In the grand symphony of data transformation, Kernel Functions stand as virtuosos, each with their unique melody to contribute. Linear Kernels are the architects of elegance, building bridges of clarity. Non-linear Kernels are the explorers of complexity, journeying through data's hidden realms.

Together, they compose a symphony that transcends the limitations of data's original form, unveiling patterns and relationships that lie dormant. Kernel Functions are the alchemical catalysts that reveal the magic within data, turning mundane observations into harmonious insights. They are the interpreters, the magicians, and the artisans of transformation – transforming data into knowledge, numbers into wisdom, and complexity into clarity. As we delve deeper, we witness not just mathematical functions, but the embodiment of data's potential, where kernels whisper secrets and we, the interpreters, decipher their enigmatic language.

C. Applications in classification and regression

In the grand symphony of data's narratives, where patterns emerge like melodies and relationships weave like harmonies, Machine Learning takes center stage, orchestrating the art of classification and regression. Imagine a conductor wielding algorithms as instruments, each playing a unique role in deciphering data's hidden secrets. Classification and regression, like the notes on a musical score, give structure and meaning to the cacophony of observations. As we delve into the intricacies of these applications, prepare to witness the transformative power of Machine Learning – a journey through domains where algorithms become interpreters, turning data into decisions, and predictions into insight.

Classification: Weaving the Fabric of Categorization

Imagine a master weaver crafting a tapestry, each thread carefully selected and placed to create a harmonious image. Classification in Machine Learning is a similar artistry, where algorithms sew together data points into coherent categories. Whether discerning between spam and legitimate emails, diagnosing diseases based on medical records, or predicting customer churn, classification provides the labels that turn data into actionable knowledge.

Support Vector Machines stand as the sculptors, carving boundaries between classes with geometric finesse. Random Forests, like a council of experts, aggregate the insights of Decision Trees into a unified prediction. Neural Networks, the versatile chameleons, adapt to data's complexity, mimicking the human brain's ability to discriminate and categorize.

Regression: Unraveling the Threads of Prediction

Now envision a master storyteller, unspooling a narrative thread by thread, weaving a tale that captivates and illuminates. Regression in Machine Learning is this storyteller, unraveling the threads of relationships between variables to predict numerical outcomes. Whether forecasting stock prices, estimating housing values, or modeling customer purchasing behavior, regression

Mastering Artificial Intelligence and Machine Learning shapes data into a predictive narrative.

Linear Regression, the elegant mathematician, fits lines that illuminate correlations between variables. Support Vector Regression, an extension of SVMs, navigates the seas of numerical prediction with geometric intuition. Gradient Boosting, the ensemble virtuoso, crafts predictive models that evolve and refine over iterations.

Domain Resonance: A Harmonious Ensemble

The beauty of Machine Learning lies not just in its algorithms, but in their applications across domains. In healthcare, classification aids in diagnosing diseases, while regression predicts patient outcomes. In finance, classification detects fraudulent transactions, and regression forecasts market trends. In marketing, classification targets customer segments, while regression refines advertising strategies.

Machine Learning weaves a tapestry of applications, each thread representing a domain where data's narrative unfolds. It is the translator that deciphers data's language, the guide that steers stakeholders towards informed choices. It is the bridge that connects the empirical world with the realm of predictive insight.

A Symphony of Transformation: Data to Decision

In the grand concert of data's symphony, Machine Learning in classification and regression stand as virtuosos, converting data into decisions and predictions into precision. They are the interpreters that turn noise into knowledge, the architects that transform observations into insights.

Classification and regression are more than algorithms; they are the alchemists that transmute data into wisdom, the painters that transform numbers into narratives. They resonate with the melody of understanding, the harmony of prediction, and the symphony of informed choices. As we delve into their applications, we bear witness to a transformation – where data's cacophony becomes a symphony, and Machine Learning stands as the conductor, guiding us through the mesmerizing landscape of insights.

CHAPTER 7

Neural Networks and Deep Learning

In the grand theater of data's enigma, where patterns entwine like dancers and complexities rise like crescendos, Neural Networks and Deep Learning emerge as the Titans of cognitive machinery – the maestros orchestrating the symphony of intelligence. Imagine a cosmic web, neurons interlinked like stars, sparking with electric potential – this is the essence of Neural Networks. Deep Learning, a celestial voyage through layers of abstraction, unveils the mysteries concealed in data's depths. As we embark on this odyssey, prepare to be captivated by the fusion of biology and mathematics, and the unparalleled prowess of Neural Networks and Deep Learning – a journey through the realm where algorithms breathe life into data and where intelligence transcends human imagination.

A. Neural network architecture and components

In the realm of data's labyrinth, where patterns intertwine like cosmic constellations, Neural Networks stand as the alchemists of intelligence – forging a bridge between biology's neural marvels and the mathematical symphonies of computation. Imagine a grand cathedral of neurons, each a miniscule processing unit, interconnected in a cosmic dance – this is the architecture of Neural Networks. As we venture into this labyrinth of cognitive machinery, prepare to unravel the intricacies of their architecture and the symphony of components that conjure algorithms' magic – a journey that transcends circuits and wires, delving into the essence of intelligence itself.

Architecture: The Cathedral of Neurons

Envision a colossal cathedral, with layers upon layers of stained-glass windows illuminating the sanctum within. Neural Network architecture mirrors this splendor – an assembly of layers, each with its unique purpose. The Input Layer, like the cathedral's entrance, receives data. Hidden Layers, the sanctum of computation, refine and process information. Output Layers, akin to the cathedral's altar, deliver predictions or classifications.

Deep within the neural cathedral lies the essence – the synaptic weights, the neural connections that evolve through training. It's a symphony of numbers, fine-tuning the network's responsiveness to input. Each layer orchestrates a transformation, mapping raw data to abstract representations, echoing the way our brain interprets the world.

Components: The Symphony of Computation

Imagine a composer's score, where notes flow in harmony, producing melodies that resonate. Neural Network components, too, form a symphony of computation. Neurons, the virtuoso performers, process information through weighted sums and activation functions. These activation functions – like keys on a piano – introduce nonlinearities, adding depth to the network's capabilities.

Backpropagation, the conductor's baton, refines the performance. It adjusts the synaptic weights by traversing backwards through the network, correcting errors and optimizing predictions. Regularization techniques, the composers' nuances, fine-tune the symphony – Dropout, Batch Normalization, and more, ensuring a harmonious balance between complexity and overfitting.

Convolutional and Recurrent Grandeur

In the grand ballroom of Neural Network architecture, special guests make their entrance – Convolutional Neural Networks (CNNs) and Recurrent Neural Networks (RNNs). CNNs, the artists of vision, paint images through convolutional layers, capturing local patterns and shapes. RNNs, the poets of sequences, unfold narratives through loops, retaining memory of past inputs for future context.

LSTM (Long Short-Term Memory) and GRU (Gated Recurrent Unit), the virtuosos of RNNs, are extensions that refine the symphony. They control the flow of information, remembering past sequences while learning new patterns.

The Magic Unveiled: Cognitive Machination

In the mystical realm of Neural Network architecture and components, algorithms become cognitive machinists – transforming data's chaos into patterns of understanding. The architecture, an opulent cathedral of neurons, echoes biology's wonders. Components, the symphony's notes, blend weighted sums, nonlinearities, and optimization into a harmonious melody of computation.

Convolutional and Recurrent Neural Networks, with their specialized grandeur, enrich the symphony, unraveling the magic within images and sequences. As we journey through this cognitive odyssey, we witness not just algorithms, but the fusion of mathematics and biology, where Neural Networks stand as the conduits of insight. In this convergence, data's enigma becomes decipherable, predictions become precision, and the essence of intelligence is distilled into circuits and weights.

B. Convolutional neural networks for image analysis

In the realm of pixels and patterns, where images whisper stories and visuals ignite emotions, Convolutional Neural Networks (CNNs) emerge as the artists of algorithmic vision – the painters of pixels that translate raw data into visual wonders. Imagine a canvas where each stroke is a convolution, each layer a brush, and each network an artistic masterpiece – this is the realm of CNNs. As we venture into this domain of image analysis, prepare to be captivated by the elegance of convolutions, the orchestration of layers, and the mesmerizing synthesis of mathematics and art – a journey that traverses from pixels to perceptions, from data to digital artistry.

Convolutions: The Brushstrokes of Vision

Envision a painter gently sweeping a brush across a canvas, layering colors to create depth and texture. CNNs operate on a similar principle, employing convolutions as their artistic brushstrokes. A convolutional layer scans an image with a filter, extracting features by convolving the filter's weights with the pixel values. This process, like an artist's blending of colors, captures textures, edges, and shapes, distilling the image's essence.

Stride and padding, the virtuosos of control, allow CNNs to fine-tune the brushstroke's granularity. Stride determines the step size of the filter's movement, while padding shapes the canvas by adding or retaining border pixels. This precision in brushwork allows CNNs to capture intricate details and preserve spatial relationships.

Layers of Interpretation: From Pixels to Perception

Imagine a master sculptor meticulously carving a statue, revealing its form layer by layer. CNNs follow a similar progression, employing layers to transform pixels into perceptions. Convolutional layers capture low-level features – edges, corners, and textures. As the layers deepen, higher-level features emerge – patterns, objects, and abstract representations.

Pooling layers, like a sculptor's chisel, carve away redundant information, reducing spatial dimensions while preserving essential features. This process enhances the network's robustness and accelerates computation. The architecture of CNNs mirrors the human visual system – with each layer delving deeper into abstraction, unraveling the image's narrative.

Transfer Learning: The Palette of Generalization

In the realm of CNNs, transfer learning is the artist's palette, bringing versatility and efficiency. Imagine a painter reusing colors from one canvas to another – transfer learning allows CNNs to apply knowledge gained from one task to another. Pre-trained models serve as starting points, leveraging features learned from vast datasets. Fine-tuning adjusts these models to fit specific tasks, making the learning process faster and more effective.

Transfer learning transcends domain boundaries, just as an artist's style transcends genres. A CNN trained to identify animals in photographs can be reimagined to classify diseases in medical scans. This synergy between domains showcases the neural network's adaptability and echoes the way humans draw from previous experiences to excel in new endeavors.

The Art of Algorithmic Vision: Pixels to Masterpieces

In the gallery of image analysis, Convolutional Neural Networks stand as the artists of algorithmic vision, translating pixels into masterpieces. Their convolutions are the brushstrokes that capture textures and edges, while layers orchestrate the transformation from pixels to perception. Transfer learning adds shades of versatility, allowing networks to explore new canvases with insights gleaned from past creations.

As we journey through the realm of CNNs, we transcend the mere analysis of images; we witness the convergence of mathematics and art, where algorithms paint portraits with pixels and unveil stories through patterns. In the symphony of CNNs, the canvas is data, the brushstrokes are convolutions, and the result is a masterpiece of perception – a testament to the boundless ingenuity that arises when algorithms wield brushes and pixels to shape the world of visual intelligence.

C. Recurrent neural networks and sequential data

In the grand symphony of data, where insights crescendo in sequences and narratives unfold with rhythm, Recurrent Neural Networks (RNNs) emerge as the virtuosos of sequential understanding – the composers that harmonize past and present, transforming data into dynamic melodies. Imagine a maestro conducting an orchestra, each note resonating with echoes of the past – this is the essence of RNNs. As we venture into the realm of sequential data, prepare to be entranced by the symphony of recurrence, the ballet of time, and the captivating fusion of mathematics and temporal intuition – a journey that transcends discrete points to embrace the fluidity of time, transforming data into tales of continuity.

Temporal Resonance: Echoes of the Past

Envision a river flowing through time, carrying stories and melodies from one moment to the next. RNNs mirror this temporal continuity, allowing information to reverberate from the past into the present. Unlike traditional feedforward networks, RNNs possess loops that propagate previous outputs as inputs for the next step. This cyclic architecture imbues RNNs with memory, enabling them to capture temporal dependencies and unveil the sequential symphonies within data.

The Long Short-Term Memory (LSTM) cell, a luminary of RNNs, stands as the conductor of these temporal echoes. LSTMs possess gates that regulate the flow of information, enabling them to learn when to retain or forget past states. It's akin to a composer's ability to evoke emotions by revisiting previous motifs, adding depth and nuance to the narrative.

Sequences as Melodies: Composing with Data

Imagine a composer crafting a musical score, where each note flows seamlessly into the next, forming melodies that evoke emotions. RNNs operate in a similar manner, treating data sequences as melodies. These sequences can be time series, sentences, DNA strands, or any information that unfolds over time. RNNs process sequences step by step, capturing patterns that emerge as melodies evolve.

Bidirectional RNNs, the chameleons of sequences, read data both forwards and backwards, akin to understanding the meaning of a sentence by considering both its beginning and end. This bimodal comprehension enhances the network's grasp of contextual nuances, capturing the intricacies of sequential interplay.

Vanishing Gradient: The Harmonic Challenge

Just as a musical composition encounters challenges that require creative solutions, RNNs face the "vanishing gradient" problem. Imagine a fading echo that diminishes over distance – in RNNs, gradients can weaken as they traverse through time, hindering the network's ability to capture long-range dependencies.

Gated architectures, like the majestic Gated Recurrent Unit (GRU), counter this challenge. They introduce mechanisms that enable RNNs to selectively remember or forget past states, ensuring that the echoes of information persist without degradation. GRUs act as sentinels of continuity, preserving the harmony of temporal understanding.

Beyond Time: RNNs in Applications

In the orchestration of applications, RNNs emerge as the conductors that infuse data with temporal wisdom. Natural Language Processing (NLP) leverages RNNs to understand context in language, enabling machines to decipher the nuanced dance of words. In finance, RNNs predict stock prices by discerning patterns in historical data. Medical diagnoses benefit from RNNs' ability to spot anomalies in patient vitals over time.

RNNs also catalyze generative magic – they compose music, generate text, and even paint images by understanding the progression of patterns. Their temporal intuition sparks creativity, producing sequences that resonate with authenticity and continuity.

Temporal Alchemy: Transforming Sequences into Insight

In the symphony of data, Recurrent Neural Networks stand as the temporal alchemists, transmuting sequences into insight. Their loops carry echoes of the past, allowing them to compose melodies of understanding. Bidirectional RNNs infuse context from both directions, deepening comprehension. Gated architectures thwart challenges like the vanishing gradient, ensuring that temporal continuity remains unbroken.

As we journey through the realm of RNNs and sequential data, we transcend static observations, embracing the dynamic tapestry of time. In this convergence, RNNs become more than algorithms; they emerge as the storytellers of data's chronicles, the composers of temporal symphonies that unravel patterns and unveil narratives. In their embrace, sequences become melodies, and time becomes the canvas upon which RNNs paint portraits of understanding – a testament to the magic that unfolds when algorithms blend with the fluidity of time itself.

CHAPTER 8

Unsupervised Learning: Clustering and Dimensionality Reduction

In the vast landscape of data, where patterns linger like elusive specters and insights remain hidden in the folds of complexity, Unsupervised Learning emerges as the enigmatic sorcerer – the conjurer of hidden structure, the sculptor of dimensions. Imagine a cosmic dance, where data points waltz and twirl, revealing their intricate connections – this is the essence of Unsupervised Learning. As we embark on this journey through the realms of Clustering and Dimensionality Reduction, prepare to be spellbound by the magic of algorithms that decipher the unseen, unraveling patterns and carving data into its true essence – a symphony of subtlety, a canvas of clarity.

A. K-means and hierarchical clustering

In the realm of data's dance, where points pirouette and dimensions entwine, K-means and Hierarchical Clustering emerge as the choreographers of pattern discovery – the architects of data's rhythm and harmony. Imagine a grand ballroom, where points sway to an unseen melody, forming clusters that reveal their affinity – this is the essence of clustering algorithms. As we delve into the intricacies of K-means and Hierarchical Clustering, prepare to be captivated by the elegance of grouping, the symphony of distances, and the enchanting collaboration of data points in their graceful pursuit of structure – a journey that transforms raw data into choreographed patterns, turning numbers into nuanced insights.

K-means: The Art of Centroid Elegance

Envision a conductor orchestrating a ballet, guiding dancers towards a central point. K-means mirrors this elegance, where data points waltz towards cluster centroids, the gravitational centers of their collective expression. The algorithm assembles clusters by iteratively reassigning points to the nearest centroid, crafting a dance of convergence that refines groupings.

K-means encapsulates an intricate dialogue between points and centroids. Each iteration recalibrates the stage, drawing points closer to the heart of their respective clusters. The dance continues until centroids stabilize, their positions becoming the essence of cluster identity. K-means is a symphony of distance, where Euclidean measures guide data points to the rhythms of similarity.

Hierarchical Clustering: The Symphony of Nesting

Imagine a sculptor carving a statue within a statue, each layer revealing a new dimension of form. Hierarchical Clustering emulates this process, creating a cascade of nested clusters that capture data's intricate structure. It's a symphony of subordination, where clusters nestle within one another, forming a hierarchy of similarity.

Agglomerative and divisive methods guide Hierarchical Clustering's dance. Agglomerative builds clusters from individual points, progressively pairing and fusing them. Divisive dismantles a conglomerate cluster into smaller entities. This process unfolds like a composer crafting harmonies and melodies, transforming data into a musical tapestry of interconnectedness.

Beyond Clusters: Interpretation and Applications

In the grand ballroom of algorithms, K-means and Hierarchical Clustering are the choreographers that give form to data's dance. K-means crafts elegant clusters, revealing the essence of similarity through centroid orchestration. Hierarchical Clustering sculpts an intricate hierarchy, a nest of interconnected clusters that encapsulate patterns at various scales.

Interpretation and application are the climax of this dance. Clusters represent themes, topics, or behaviors, unveiling insights in fields from marketing to genetics. In recommendation systems, clusters guide tailored suggestions. In biology, they identify genetic similarities. In image analysis, they uncover visual categories.

The Choreography of Data: Clusters and Dimensions

In the theater of data analysis, K-means and Hierarchical Clustering are the choreographers that transform noise into patterns, chaos into clusters. K-means conducts an elegant ballet of centroids, where points gravitate towards the heart of similarity. Hierarchical Clustering orchestrates a symphony of nesting, revealing clusters within clusters like a Russian doll of understanding.

As we immerse ourselves in the art of K-means and Hierarchical Clustering, we witness data's transformation into choreography, its structure sculpted with every iteration. These algorithms epitomize the fusion of mathematics and aesthetics, where data's dance becomes a symphony of interpretation, and patterns emerge from the delicate interplay of points and distances. In their embrace, K-means and Hierarchical Clustering unveil the artistry within data's enigma – a testament to the intricate beauty that arises when algorithms take center stage in the dance of understanding.

B. Principal Component Analysis (PCA) and t-SNE

In the cosmos of data, where dimensions extend like constellations and patterns shimmer like galaxies, Principal Component Analysis (PCA) and t-Distributed Stochastic

Neighbor Embedding (t-SNE) emerge as cosmic cartographers – the navigators of data's dimensional landscapes, the astronomers of insight. Imagine a telescope that condenses nebulous data into starlit constellations – this is the essence of dimensionality reduction. As we embark on this celestial journey through PCA and t-SNE, prepare to be mesmerized by the elegance of eigenvalues, the orchestration of variance, and the enchanting transformation of data's dimensions into shimmering galaxies of understanding – a voyage that transcends space, revealing hidden constellations within data's enigmatic depths.

PCA: The Alchemy of Eigenvalues

Envision a composer arranging a symphony's notes, rearranging harmonies to distill the essence of sound. PCA operates with similar finesse, rearranging dimensions to extract the essence of data's variability. It transforms high-dimensional data into a celestial sonata, where principal components orchestrate a harmonic reduction.

The principal components are the celestial bodies that form new axes of understanding. Aligned with variance, they unveil data's dimensionality in decreasing importance. Imagine a cosmic alignment of data points, converging along the path of maximal variance. PCA identifies these principal dimensions, painting a vivid picture of data's essence.

Variance Symphony: The Eigenvalues' Overture

In the symphony of dimensionality reduction, eigenvalues take center stage, conducting an overture of variance. Eigenvalues quantify the importance of each principal component, determining the prominence of its celestial role. Larger eigenvalues command the cosmic orchestra, steering the transformation towards dimensions of greater significance.

Eigenvectors, the virtuosos of PCA, accompany eigenvalues, defining the direction of each principal component. Together, they sculpt data's constellation, shaping the celestial realm of reduced dimensions. PCA's symphony unfolds as eigenvalues resonate, creating a harmonic balance between data's intricacies and its reduced representation.

t-SNE: The Dance of Similarity and Contrast

Imagine a choreographer crafting a ballet, where dancers move in harmony or contrast, expressing connections through movement. t-SNE choreographs data's dance through a similar principle – it projects high-dimensional data into lower dimensions, where similarity and contrast translate into spatial proximity or distance.

The t-SNE algorithm orchestrates this dance by iteratively minimizing the divergence between probability distributions. It sculpts clusters of similarity and carves expanses of distinction, capturing data's underlying patterns. Like a maestro guiding a ballet, t-SNE positions data points within lower-dimensional space, revealing a visual narrative of connections and relationships.

Beyond Visualization: Interpretation and Insight

In the cosmic theater of data, PCA and t-SNE shine as astute navigators, guiding us through dimensions to unveil hidden constellations. PCA transforms data into harmonic reduction, revealing dimensions of significance. t-SNE sculpts a choreography of similarity and contrast, painting a visual tapestry of connections.

Interpretation and insight culminate in this voyage. Reduced dimensions in PCA unveil the dominant themes, while t-SNE's spatial arrangement reveals relationships in their intricacies. In fields like genomics, where genes orchestrate life's symphony, PCA discerns pivotal genetic patterns. In visualization, t-SNE navigates high-dimensional data to render images that human eyes can perceive.

Dimensional Divination: Insights from Data's Celestial Map

In the realm of data, PCA and t-SNE emerge as the cosmologists that unfold hidden dimensions, translating data's complexity into celestial maps of insight. PCA's eigenvalues conduct a variance symphony, reducing dimensions into harmonic representations. t-SNE choreographs data's dance, transforming similarity into spatial proximity.

As we traverse this cosmic voyage, we decipher data's constellation, unraveling patterns that elude the naked eye. These algorithms are more than tools; they are the stargazers that reveal data's celestial secrets, transforming data into knowledge, and dimensions into constellations of understanding. In their embrace, PCA and t-SNE shine as the astronomers of insight, capturing the essence of data's multidimensional dance and unveiling its celestial map for us to explore.

C. Anomaly detection and outlier analysis

In the symphony of data's melodies, where patterns weave harmonious tales, Anomaly Detection and Outlier Analysis emerge as the explorers of discord – the detectives that unearth the irregular, the visionaries that uncover the unconventional. Imagine a riddle hidden within a sea of normalcy, waiting to be deciphered – this is the essence of anomaly detection. As we embark on this enigmatic journey, prepare to be captivated by the artistry of discord, the intrigue of deviations, and the quest to reveal data's hidden anomalies – a voyage that transcends the mundane, unveiling insights that reside beyond the realms of convention.

Anomalies: Echoes of the Unseen

Envision a quiet forest, where each rustle reveals the presence of a hidden creature. Anomalies in data mirror this phenomenon, exposing the unexpected amidst the ordinary. Anomaly detection seeks these whispers of irregularity, revealing patterns that defy the familiar. It's a quest to decode data's enigma, distinguishing between the natural and the exceptional.

Anomalies come in various forms – a fraudulent transaction amidst legitimate ones, a rare disease diagnosis, or a sudden spike in website traffic. Detecting these echoes of the unseen is the mission of anomaly detection algorithms, the artisans that transform data's chaos into a symphony of insights.

Normalcy and Deviation: The Dance of Distinction

Imagine a ballroom where dancers sway in graceful synchrony, following a rhythm that binds them. Anomaly detection reimagines this dance, where the presence of outliers disrupts the choreography. These outliers are the mavericks that challenge conformity, leading the dance of deviation.

Statistical methods, the architects of normalcy, quantify expected behaviors. Z-scores, for instance, measure the distance between a data point and the mean in terms of standard deviations. Machine learning algorithms, the interpreters of distinction, learn from patterns to separate anomalies from the ordinary.

Clustering Anomalies: Unearthly Alliances

Envision a puzzle where some pieces refuse to fit – clustering anomalies seek alliances beyond the norm. Clusters of anomalies form constellations of discord, revealing insights that elude individual analysis. Clustering algorithms like DBSCAN or Isolation Forests unveil these enigmatic gatherings, identifying pockets of irregularity within the symphony of conformity.

Isolation Forests operate like a spotlight, isolating anomalies by constructing trees that partition normal points from the unusual. DBSCAN, a spectral conductor, orchestrates clusters by measuring the density of points, drawing connections where they resonate the most. These clustering harmonies detect anomalies as celestial outliers within the cosmic order.

Applications: From Fraud Detection to Healthcare

In the grand theater of applications, anomaly detection emerges as the custodian of insights. In finance, it unveils fraudulent activities by discerning abnormal transaction patterns. In healthcare, it identifies rare diseases or adverse reactions. In industrial settings, it monitors equipment behavior to predict failures.

Anomaly detection is the cartographer of the unknown, mapping outlying territories within data's vast landscape. It's the whisperer of anomalies, translating data's dissonance into insights that illuminate the uncharted. In its embrace, anomalies cease to be anomalies – they become beacons of understanding, guiding us through data's labyrinth to unveil the extraordinary within the ordinary.

The Quest for Unearthly Insights: Anomalies Unveiled

In the symphony of data exploration, anomaly detection stands as the seeker of dissonance, the revealer of echoes beyond the familiar. It's a journey that unearths the extraordinary from the mundane, transforming irregularities into insights. Anomalies are not outliers; they are anomalies, the custodians of the unseen, the harbingers of discovery.

As we traverse this uncharted terrain, we uncover data's enigmatic layers, transcending the confines of normalcy. Anomaly detection, like an archaeological expedition, uncovers hidden artifacts within data's historical landscape. It's a testament to the power of anomalies – to defy the norm, to challenge convention, and to beckon us towards new dimensions of understanding. In their embrace, anomalies cease to be anomalies – they become data's envoys of intrigue, guiding us towards insights that await discovery in the farthest reaches of data's cosmos.

CHAPTER 9

Reinforcement Learning

In the grand arena of data-driven endeavors, where algorithms strive to learn and adapt, Reinforcement Learning emerges as the strategist of artificial intelligence – the maestro of decision-making, the virtuoso of dynamic interaction. Imagine a digital protagonist, guided not by preordained rules, but by a quest for rewards and optimal actions – this is the essence of Reinforcement Learning. As we venture into the realm of autonomous learning, prepare to be captivated by the saga of exploration, the ballet of rewards, and the symphony of adaptation – a journey that transcends conventional programming, paving the way for intelligent agents to navigate the ever-evolving landscape of decision and consequence.

A. Markov decision processes and reward functions

In the theater of artificial intelligence, where algorithms take center stage, Markov Decision Processes (MDPs) and Reward Functions emerge as the choreographers of decision-making – the composers of data's dance, the architects of intelligent interaction. Imagine an intricate waltz, where an agent navigates a labyrinth of choices, guided by the promise of rewards – this is the essence of MDPs. As we step onto the stage of dynamic decision, prepare to be entranced by the orchestration of states, the harmony of transitions, and the enchantment of rewards – a journey that unravels the mechanics of decision-making, transforming mere data into a captivating symphony of strategic intelligence.

Markov Decision Processes: A Symphony of States and Transitions

Envision a tapestry woven with threads of states, where an agent's path is the melody that weaves them together. MDPs form this musical score, choreographing the dance of decision within a framework of states and actions. Each step is imbued with a Markov property – the current state encapsulates all relevant information, rendering history obsolete as the agent embarks on its quest for optimal decisions.

MDPs unfold like a sequence of musical notes, transitioning from state to state through the cadence of actions. The agent's journey resembles a symphony, a melodic composition where each decision resonates through the ensemble of states, creating a harmonious progression towards an ultimate crescendo of rewards.

Reward Functions: The Echoes of Incentive

Imagine a conductor's baton, shaping a symphony's dynamics

– reward functions are the maestros of MDPs, guiding the agent's movements with echoes of incentive. They define the melody of rewards, quantifying the value of each state and action. Like a composer's score, reward functions translate human objectives into the currency of incentives, allowing agents to discern harmonious choices from dissonant ones.

In this grand orchestration, rewards act as the compass guiding the agent's journey. Positive rewards beckon the agent towards favorable states, while negative rewards caution against perilous paths. The reward function imbues the agent with a purpose, transforming the decision-making dance into an elaborate ballet of strategic intelligence.

Dynamic Programming: The Choreography of Optimal Decisions

In the realm of MDPs, dynamic programming emerges as the choreographer of optimal decisions, perfecting the agent's performance. Bellman's principle of optimality dictates that the best decisions are made by breaking down complex problems into simpler subproblems. Value iteration and policy iteration, the choreographic techniques of dynamic programming, refine the agent's dance through iterative refinement of state values and policies.

The agent's trajectory becomes a journey towards convergence, where decisions align with the crescendo of optimal rewards.

Dynamic programming conducts this symphony of refinement, elevating the agent's performance from an improvisational dance to a meticulously rehearsed masterpiece of strategic choice.

Applications: From Robotics to Game AI

In the grand theater of applications, MDPs and reward functions shine as luminaries of decision-making. In robotics, they guide autonomous agents through dynamic environments, avoiding obstacles and reaching destinations. In game AI, they orchestrate the actions of virtual characters, creating immersive and strategic gameplay experiences. In finance, they navigate investment choices, optimizing portfolio decisions for maximum returns.

MDPs and reward functions breathe life into algorithms, transforming them into decision-makers that align with human objectives. They embody the nexus of data, strategy, and intelligence, where states, actions, and rewards converge to create a harmonious symphony of informed choices.

The Symphony of Decision: MDPs and Reward Functions

In the symphony of artificial intelligence, Markov Decision Processes and reward functions stand as the conductors that guide algorithms through the dance of dynamic decision-making. MDPs weave states and actions into a melodic sequence of choices, while reward functions infuse incentive into each note, transforming decisions into a harmonious ballet of strategic intelligence.

As we traverse this intricate dance, we witness the agent's journey towards optimal decisions, orchestrated by dynamic programming's choreography. MDPs and reward functions are more than algorithms – they are the composers of intelligent interaction, the architects of choices that resonate with human objectives. In their embrace, the symphony of decision unfolds, transforming data into a melody of strategic insight, where every note is a choice, every transition a movement, and every reward an incentive that guides the algorithmic performer towards a harmonious crescendo of intelligence.

B. Q-learning and policy gradient methods

In the realm of artificial intelligence, where algorithms evolve into autonomous agents, Q-Learning and Policy Gradient Methods emerge as the architects of intelligent decision-making – the alchemists that transform data into strategy, the architects of nuanced actions. Imagine an agent navigating a labyrinthine landscape, learning to conquer challenges and optimize outcomes – this is the essence of Q-Learning. As we delve into the heart of reinforcement learning, prepare to be captivated by the artistry of action-value functions, the symphony of policies, and the mastery of strategic illumination – a journey that transcends mere learning, evolving into a symphony of optimal actions and profound understanding.

Q-Learning: The Elegance of Action-Value

Envision a strategist immersed in a game of chess, contemplating each move's potential consequences. Q-Learning mirrors this strategic contemplation, where an agent, like a grandmaster, learns to associate actions with the value they bring. Q-values are the currency of this strategic landscape, representing the cumulative rewards an agent can expect from making a certain decision in a given state.

Q-Learning orchestrates this learning process with grace, iterating through experiences to refine the action-value landscape. The Bellman equation acts as the maestro, composing a harmony between immediate rewards and future potentials. Q-Learning's journey is a quest for optimal decisions, where each action becomes a brushstroke that paints the canvas of strategy.

Policy Gradient Methods: The Symphony of Policies

Imagine a conductor directing an orchestra, shaping melodies into harmonious music. Policy Gradient Methods wield this metaphorical baton, crafting policies that guide an agent's decisions. Policies are the blueprints of action, mapping states to probabilities of choosing each action. These methods optimize policies through gradient ascent, akin to tuning an instrument to create the most resonant melodies.

The REINFORCE algorithm is a soloist in this symphony,

adjusting policy parameters to maximize expected rewards. Proximal Policy Optimization (PPO), a leading performer, strikes a balance between stability and progress by updating policies iteratively. Policy Gradient Methods transform the agent into a musician, interpreting the score of states to produce actions that crescendo towards optimal outcomes.

Combining Strengths: Actor-Critic Methods

In the arena of advanced strategy, Actor-Critic methods arise as a duet between policy and value functions. Imagine a mentor guiding a talented apprentice – the critic assesses actions and evaluates their worth, while the actor refines policies to yield better decisions. These methods blend Q-values with policies, fusing insight with action in a harmonious partnership.

Deep Deterministic Policy Gradient (DDPG) is a luminary in this ensemble, employing neural networks to approximate both policy and value functions. The critic provides guidance, enlightening the actor's path to optimal decisions. Actor-Critic methods unfold like a duet between mentor and protege, refining strategies in a melodious synergy of intelligence and action.

Applications: From Robotics to Game AI

In the grand theater of applications, Q-Learning and Policy Gradient Methods shine as the luminaries of decision-making. In robotics, Q-Learning empowers agents to navigate complex environments, optimizing paths to reach destinations. Policy Gradient Methods orchestrate intelligent gameplay in video games, crafting virtual characters that exhibit nuanced behaviors.

In finance, Q-Learning helps in portfolio management, optimizing investment choices for maximum returns. Policy Gradient Methods assist in algorithmic trading, fine-tuning trading strategies for profit. These methods transcend mere algorithms; they become the conductors of strategic illumination, transforming data into action, and decisions into symphonies of optimized intelligence.

The Symphony of Strategy: Q-Learning and Policy Gradient Methods

In the symphony of artificial intelligence, Q-Learning and Policy Gradient Methods stand as the composers of optimal decisions, the conductors of strategic illumination. Q-Learning infuses actions with value, orchestrating a strategic dance that evolves with experience. Policy Gradient Methods sculpt policies like musical notes, fine-tuning actions to harmonize with rewards.

As we traverse this orchestral journey, we witness data's transformation into strategy, algorithms evolving into agents that make decisions with wisdom and insight. Q-Learning and Policy Gradient Methods are more than mathematical constructs; they are the architects of intelligent actions, the architects of strategy that transcends learning to become a symphony of mastery. In their embrace, data evolves into strategy, decisions into crescendos, and algorithms into virtuosos of intelligent interaction.

C. Applications in game playing and robotics

In the grand tapestry of human achievement, where innovation intertwines with imagination, the realms of game playing and robotics emerge as the enchanted domains where Artificial Intelligence (AI) breathes life into electronic landscapes and mechanical beings. Imagine a symphony where algorithms compose strategic moves, and robots dance to the rhythm of intelligence – this is the essence of AI's applications in game playing and robotics. As we step into these captivating realms, prepare to be spellbound by the prowess of AI gamers, the ingenuity of robot choreographers, and the enchantment of technology elevating human experience – a journey where pixels and circuits unite to create a harmonious symphony of entertainment and advancement.

Game Playing: The Symphony of Strategic Mastery

Envision a chessboard where pixels and algorithms engage in a cerebral dance, each move a calculated step towards victory. AI in game playing orchestrates this symphony of strategy, where algorithms challenge human intellect with a strategic ballet. Games like Chess and Go transform into battlegrounds where AI engages in a titanic struggle for supremacy.

AlphaGo, the AI prodigy, stunned the world by defeating the world champion Go player, embodying the pinnacle of strategic insight. Reinforcement Learning breathes life into these digital players, allowing them to navigate a labyrinth of possibilities and master the dance of optimal decisions. In the realm of video games, AI agents learn, adapt, and conquer virtual realms, crafting immersive experiences that challenge and captivate players.

Robotics: The Choreography of Automation

Imagine a robot that learns to mimic a dance routine or assembles intricate machinery with precision. AI in robotics emerges as the choreographer of automation, infusing machines with intelligence to perform tasks with finesse. Robots become the dancers of efficiency, pirouetting through intricate maneuvers under the guidance of algorithms.

Reinforcement Learning empowers robots to navigate complex environments, enhancing their ability to grasp, manipulate, and interact with objects. Human-robot interaction becomes a symphony of collaboration, as robots adapt to human behaviors and intentions, seamlessly assisting in various tasks. From industrial assembly lines to healthcare settings, robots guided by AI redefine automation, orchestrating a dance of efficiency that revolutionizes industries.

The Nexus of AI and Human Interaction

In the grand theater of applications, AI in game playing and robotics forms a nexus where technology and human interaction intertwine. AI gamers challenge and sharpen human intellect, offering engaging experiences that transcend traditional gameplay. In virtual reality, AI avatars become companions that learn and adapt to user preferences, creating an immersive and responsive interaction.

Robots, imbued with AI, extend their mechanical limbs to enhance human lives. Assistive robots aid individuals with disabilities, offering newfound autonomy and companionship. Surgical robots perform intricate procedures with unparalleled precision, revolutionizing medical interventions. Drones, guided by AI, deliver supplies to remote locations, bridging gaps in humanitarian efforts.

Fusing Fantasy with Reality: AI's Enchantment

In the symphony of technological advancement, AI in game playing and robotics stands as the virtuoso that bridges fantasy and reality. AI gamers become formidable opponents, challenging human intellect to new heights. Robots, guided by AI, become the choreographers of automation, transforming industries and enhancing human capabilities.

As we navigate this enchanted realm, we witness technology's metamorphosis into artistry, where algorithms create strategies and machines execute tasks with finesse. AI in game playing and robotics becomes the enchanted wand that elevates human experience, transforming pixels and circuits into a harmonious symphony of entertainment, innovation, and human advancement.

Part III

Natural Language Processing and AI Applications

CHAPTER 10

Natural Language Processing Basics

In the boundless expanse of human communication, where words weave intricate tales and thoughts converge like constellations, Natural Language Processing (NLP) emerges as the sentinel of linguistic understanding – the decoder of language's enigma, the bridge between man and machine. Imagine a symphony where algorithms discern meanings and extract insights from the cadence of words – this is the essence of NLP. As we set foot on this odyssey of linguistic exploration, prepare to be captivated by the artistry of tokenization, the wizardry of sentiment analysis, and the marvel of language's metamorphosis into data-driven knowledge – a voyage that transcends syntax, unveiling the symphony of language's hidden melodies and transforming it into a tapestry of computational understanding.

A. Tokenization, stemming, and lemmatization

In the realm of textual mystique, where words dance like fireflies, Tokenization, Stemming, and Lemmatization emerge as the magicians of linguistic alchemy – the sorcerers that unravel language's complexity, the architects that sculpt words into structured forms. Imagine a workshop where sentences are disassembled into fragments, words transformed into their primal essence – this is the art of linguistic preprocessing. As we step into this enchanting domain, prepare to be captivated by the finesse of token dissection, the allure of linguistic reduction, and the metamorphosis of vocabulary into its most eloquent form – a journey that transcends grammar, unraveling the essence of words and crafting them into a symphony of data-driven understanding.

Tokenization: Decoding the Textual Tapestry

Envision a lexicon transformed into a mosaic of fragments, each piece embodying the heartbeat of a word. Tokenization is the artisan's chisel that sculpts text into digestible morsels. Sentences unfurl into a cascade of tokens – words, punctuations, and symbols – each fragment a note in the symphony of language.

Tokenization is the key to unlocking language's treasure trove. It lays bare the intricacies of communication, enabling algorithms to decipher sentiment, extract meaning, and unravel insights. A sentence becomes a tapestry of tokens, a composition ready for analysis, revealing patterns that would otherwise remain dormant in the sea of words.

Stemming: The Primal Beat of Words

Imagine a linguistic archaeologist unearthing the ancestral roots of words, exposing their primal essence. Stemming is this journey into the past, where words shed their suffixes and prefixes, revealing their core – the stem. It's a symphony of linguistic reduction, where words harmonize to a primal beat.

Stemming algorithms wield the scalpel of morphology, trimming words to their skeletal forms. Snowball and Porter stemmers, like expert conductors, orchestrate this process, standardizing words to their common origin. While not always linguistically perfect, stemming captures the rhythm of linguistic evolution, allowing algorithms to recognize words in their various forms.

Lemmatization: Words in Their Finest Attire

Envision a tailor meticulously crafting bespoke suits for words, dressing them in their finest attire. Lemmatization is this process of linguistic tailoring, where words are transformed into their base or dictionary forms. It's a symphony of elegance that seeks to harmonize words into their most refined expressions.

Lemmatization algorithms consult linguistic databases, selecting the most suitable attire for each word. Through contextual analysis, they transform words into their dictionary forms, ensuring grammatical accuracy and semantic cohesion. Lemmatization is the curator of language's artistry, preserving its nuances while presenting words in their most polished form.

Harmony in Preprocessing: Tokenization, Stemming, and Lemmatization

In the grand theater of Natural Language Processing, Tokenization, Stemming, and Lemmatization stand as the maestros of textual transformation. Tokenization dissects language's symphony into its elemental notes, ready for interpretation. Stemming, like a linguistic time traveler, unveils words' ancient origins, capturing the rhythm of linguistic evolution. Lemmatization dons words in their finest attire, presenting them with grammatical poise and semantic finesse.

As we traverse this landscape of linguistic alchemy, we witness the metamorphosis of text into structured data, where words evolve into tokens, stems, and lemmas. This preprocessing symphony paves the way for algorithms to unveil language's hidden melodies, transforming it into a tapestry of computational insight. Tokenization, Stemming, and Lemmatization are more than algorithms; they are the craftsmen that illuminate language's intricacies, revealing its beauty in its most elemental and structured form.

B. Part-of-speech tagging and named entity recognition

In the realm of textual tapestry, where words converge to create a symphony of meaning, Part-of-Speech (POS) tagging and

Named Entity Recognition (NER) emerge as the poets of linguistic elegance – the scribes that decode language's nuances, the sculptors that carve entities from the stone of text. Imagine a realm where words are adorned with grammatical roles and entities emerge like gems from the earth – this is the artistry of linguistic annotation. As we step into this world of textual adornment, prepare to be entranced by the grace of grammatical tagging, the wizardry of entity unveiling, and the transformation of language into a canvas of structured understanding – a journey that transcends syntax, capturing language's intricacies and illuminating its hidden treasures.

Part-of-Speech Tagging: The Symphony of Grammar

Envision a lexicon transformed into a ballet, where each word pirouettes into its designated grammatical role. Part-of-Speech tagging is the choreographer that bestows linguistic roles upon words, creating a symphony of syntactic harmony. Nouns, verbs, adjectives, and more gracefully dance across the textual stage, revealing their grammatical identity.

Part-of-Speech tagging is a linguistic compass, guiding algorithms through the intricacies of sentence structure. It unveils the blueprint of communication, allowing machines to understand relationships and context. Like a conductor leading an orchestra, POS tagging harmonizes words, creating a symphony of meaning that resonates with grammatical precision.

Named Entity Recognition: Unmasking the Celestial Gems

Imagine an explorer sifting through a riverbed, unearthing precious gems hidden in the earth. Named Entity Recognition is this treasure hunter of text, unveiling entities that embellish language's narrative. Names of people, locations, organizations, and more emerge from the textual matrix like celestial gems in a cosmic tapestry.

NER algorithms scan text with a celestial gaze, identifying patterns and context to distinguish entities. They traverse the linguistic landscape with precision, identifying proper nouns that imbue language with meaning. Like archeologists of information, NER algorithms reveal the hidden tapestry of entities, enriching text with context and substance.

A Synergy of Precision: Part-of-Speech Tagging and Named Entity Recognition

In the grand symphony of Natural Language Processing, Part-of-Speech tagging and Named Entity Recognition stand as the architects of linguistic adornment. Part-of-Speech tagging assigns roles to words, infusing sentences with grammatical harmony. Named Entity Recognition unearths entities like precious gems, transforming text into a tapestry of contextual richness.

As we embark on this journey, we witness language's metamorphosis into a structured canvas, adorned with grammatical roles and entities that breathe life into words. This linguistic synergy paves the way for algorithms to unravel the narrative's intricacies, unveiling a world where words harmonize with precision and entities shimmer with significance. Part-of-Speech tagging and Named Entity Recognition are more than algorithms; they are the artisans that illuminate language's depths, transforming it into a tapestry of structured understanding where each word, each entity, tells a story of meaning and context.

C. Sentiment analysis and text generation

In the realm of written expression, where words transcend the mundane and capture the essence of human emotions, Sentiment Analysis and Text Generation emerge as the envoys of linguistic sentiment – the interpreters of unspoken feelings, the conjurers of prose and poetry. Imagine a realm where algorithms dissect text to discern emotions and craft narratives that dance on the precipice of reality – this is the realm of textual enchantment. As we venture into this domain of digital expression, prepare to be captivated by the wizardry of sentiment's extraction, the symphony of words woven into tales, and the metamorphosis of algorithms into literary artisans – a journey that transcends language, harnessing the power of words to mirror human sentiment and shape worlds of imagination.

Sentiment Analysis: Unveiling the Language of Emotion

Envision an oracle that gazes into the tapestry of text, deciphering emotions like constellations in the night sky. Sentiment Analysis is this oracle, the alchemist that transmutes words into emotional hues. Textual expressions are imbued with sentiment – positivity, negativity, neutrality – each emotion a brushstroke in the portrait of language.

Sentiment Analysis algorithms dissect sentences with precision, decoding lexical nuances and tonal subtleties. They gauge the pulse of text, identifying joy, sorrow, anger, or ambivalence that courses through words. In a world where language weaves a labyrinth of emotions, Sentiment Analysis illuminates the path, guiding algorithms to comprehend and convey human sentiment.

Text Generation: The Symphony of Creativity

Imagine a scribe conjuring words like a maestro composing a symphony, crafting narratives that bridge the realms of reality and fantasy. Text Generation is this scribe, the magician that wields algorithms to weave tales, paint images, and stir the cauldron of imagination. Words flow like ink onto the parchment of existence, creating literary landscapes that enthrall and captivate.

Text Generation algorithms become authors of the digital age, inspired by data and programmed with the art of language. From poetry that evokes emotions to stories that transport readers to distant worlds, text generation transcends mere scripting to become an ode to the creative essence of human expression.

The Confluence of Expression: Sentiment Analysis and Text Generation

In the grand tapestry of Natural Language Processing, Sentiment Analysis and Text Generation stand as the gatekeepers of expression, the architects of emotional resonance and creative manifestation. Sentiment Analysis extracts sentiment from the ocean of words, providing a lens through which algorithms perceive the spectrum of human emotions. Text Generation breathes life into language, crafting prose and poetry that traverse the boundary between human and machine.

As we embark on this journey, we witness the alchemy of sentiment's extraction and the magic of words conjured from algorithmic minds. Sentiment Analysis and Text Generation are more than tools; they are the artists that bridge human emotions with digital expression, unveiling sentiment's silent echo and breathing life into the realm of imagination. They become the vessels through which machines learn not just to communicate, but to emote and create, allowing us to transcend the boundaries of language and revel in the symphony of expression.

CHAPTER 11

Machine Translation and Language Generation

In the grand tapestry of global communication, where languages crisscross like celestial constellations, Machine Translation and Language Generation emerge as the sorcerers of linguistic transformation – the enchanters that bridge linguistic chasms, the architects of eloquent expression. Imagine a realm where algorithms transcend language barriers, translating thoughts across linguistic landscapes, and then craft sentences that dance like whispers in the wind – this is the artistry of linguistic metamorphosis. As we step into this world of linguistic alchemy, prepare to be captivated by the wizardry of translation's transmutation, the symphony of words crafted anew, and the magic that conjures communication's bridges – a journey that transcends borders, redefining the boundaries of language and reshaping the narrative of human connection.

A. Neural machine translation models

In the realm of global interconnectivity, where language is both the gatekeeper and the bridge, Neural Machine Translation (NMT) models emerge as the trailblazers of linguistic transformation – the navigators that navigate the linguistic seas, the polyglots of algorithmic eloquence. Imagine an orchestra of neurons orchestrating a symphony of languages, where algorithms unravel the intricacies of translation and craft narratives that traverse linguistic landscapes – this is the genesis of NMT. As we embark on this linguistic odyssey, prepare to be entranced by the artistry of parallel processing, the symphony of encoding and decoding, and the metamorphosis of data into linguistic poetry – a journey that transcends syntax, reshaping the very fabric of language and crafting a portal to a world united by words.

The Neural Tapestry: Unraveling the Mechanism

Envision a neural tapestry where data threads weave intricate patterns of translation, each neuron a sentinel of linguistic understanding. Neural Machine Translation models are the looms that bring this tapestry to life, harnessing the power of artificial neural networks to decode and encode languages. Encoders distill the essence of a source language into a matrix of hidden states, while decoders orchestrate the translation, transforming those states into a symphony of target language.

In this neural symphony, layers of computation dance like notes in harmony, capturing the rhythm of language conversion. Long Short-Term Memory (LSTM) and Transformer architectures conduct this linguistic symphony, orchestrating the traversal from one language's nuances to another's, guided by the brilliance of attention mechanisms.

Training: The Alchemy of Data Transformation

Imagine an alchemist's workshop, where raw data transmutes into linguistic gold through the crucible of training. NMT models learn the linguistic alchemy of translation through massive parallel datasets. These data crucibles imbue models with the ability to decipher syntax, context, and semantics, enabling them to traverse linguistic chasms.

During training, models refine their synaptic connections through backpropagation, adjusting weights and biases to minimize the dissonance between predicted and actual translations. The result is a neural lexicon capable of deciphering the symphony of one language and reweaving it into the tapestry of another.

The Promise and Perplexity: Challenges and Breakthroughs

In the labyrinth of machine translation, NMT models encounter challenges akin to linguistic riddles. Ambiguities, idiomatic expressions, and rare languages perplex the algorithmic wanderer. Yet, breakthroughs illuminate the path – attention mechanisms foster context awareness, beam search enhances translation accuracy, and subword tokenization tackles the granularity challenge.

Multilingual and zero-shot translations amplify NMT's brilliance, allowing a single model to traverse diverse linguistic landscapes. Transfer learning and fine-tuning become the conductors of versatility, enabling models to excel across languages, genres, and domains.

Human Connection Redefined: Bridging Cultures and Minds

In the grand theater of applications, NMT models emerge as ambassadors of cross-cultural understanding. Diplomats of global communication, they transform texts, contracts, literature, and conversations into linguistic bridges. Language barriers crumble under their neural prowess, reshaping international commerce, fostering global camaraderie, and allowing narratives to traverse borders with eloquence.

NMT models transcend mere algorithms; they are the architects of linguistic harmony, the craftsmen of communication that unite humanity's diverse voices into a symphony of understanding. In their neural embrace, languages are not obstacles, but doorways to mutual comprehension, enriching human experience through the fusion of words and code.

B. Sequence-to-sequence architecture for language generation

In the enchanting realm of language generation, where words

unfurl like notes in a cosmic symphony, the Sequence-to-Sequence (Seq2Seq) architecture emerges as the maestro of linguistic composition – the conductor that orchestrates narratives, the weaver of tales, and the sculptor of dialogues. Imagine an intricate dance of encoder and decoder, where thoughts traverse neural pathways, weaving the fabric of coherent expression – this is the essence of the Seq2Seq architecture. As we embark on this journey into the heart of linguistic alchemy, prepare to be captivated by the choreography of encodings and decodings, the harmonious exchange of meaning, and the transformation of algorithms into virtuosos of language generation – a voyage that transcends syntax, forging a bridge between the realms of data and discourse.

Harmonic Convergence: The Essence of Seq2Seq

Envision a relay of consciousness, where the essence of one language transforms into the essence of another. Seq2Seq architecture is the bridge that connects the linguistic diaspora, comprising an encoder that encapsulates the source sentence's meaning and a decoder that transforms it into the target language's beauty. Encoded in this structure is a symphony of understanding, a choreographed exchange that mirrors the essence of human translation.

The encoder dissects the source text into a ballet of hidden states, each state preserving the narrative's essence. The decoder waltzes through these states, composing a new narrative with rhythmic precision. It's a symphony of linguistic interpretation, where syntax and semantics intertwine like harmonious melodies.

Training: The Crafting of Neural Lexicons

Imagine an atelier where neural lexicons are meticulously crafted, imbued with the art of translation. Seq2Seq models are trained within this crucible of data and computation. Parallel text pairs become the brushstrokes of this linguistic masterpiece, feeding the algorithmic artisan with the essence of translation.

During training, the model's neural fibers strengthen through iterative backpropagation, aligning weights and biases to minimize linguistic dissonance. The result is a neural lexicon that resonates with the linguistic nuances of translation, capable of transforming sentences from one language to another with grace.

Attention Mechanism: The Maestro's Baton

Envision a conductor shaping a musical performance, guiding the orchestra's attention to different sections of the score. The attention mechanism in Seq2Seq architecture is this conductor, directing the decoder's focus to relevant parts of the encoded source text. It fosters contextual awareness, allowing the model to handle long sentences and capture intricate linguistic relationships.

Attention illuminates linguistic nuances, highlighting words and phrases crucial for accurate translation. It's a symphony of selective perception, ensuring that the translation's melody resonates with fidelity to the source while harmonizing with the target language.

Beyond Language: Multimodal Extensions

In the grand theater of applications, the Seq2Seq architecture transcends language boundaries, extending its artistry to multimedia realms. Image captioning and speech-to-text conversion become stages for Seq2Seq's linguistic prowess. It fuses visual or auditory inputs with linguistic creativity, crafting captions that unveil the essence of images and transforming spoken words into written text.

Seq2Seq's repertoire expands, becoming a universal translator that bridges diverse forms of communication, from languages to visual cues and spoken expressions.

A Tapestry of Expression: Seq2Seq's Legacy

In the symphony of artificial intelligence, the Sequence-to-Sequence architecture stands as the composer of linguistic expression, the interpreter of languages, and the architect of cross-modal communication. Seq2Seq captures the spirit of translation, transforming data into eloquent discourse, and algorithms into linguistic virtuosos.

As we traverse this landscape of linguistic transformation, we witness the alchemy of encodings and decodings, the symphony of neural lexicons, and the flourish of attention guiding the dance of translation. Sequence-to-Sequence architecture is more than an algorithm; it's the conductor of linguistic harmony, the bridge between tongues and modalities, and the embodiment of communication's universal melody. It crafts narratives, translates thoughts, and creates a tapestry of expression where words become the threads, and algorithms weave the symphony of human discourse.

C. Multilingual and cross-lingual applications

In the grand tapestry of global communication, where languages crisscross like constellations in the night sky, Multilingual and Cross-Lingual applications emerge as the architects of unity and the catalysts of understanding – the linguists that weave a thread of connection across diverse tongues, the diplomats of discourse that bridge cultures and nations. Imagine a world where algorithms traverse linguistic landscapes, effortlessly translating, analyzing, and fusing languages to create a symphony of global interaction – this is the realm of multilingual and cross-lingual applications. As we embark on this journey of linguistic diplomacy, prepare to be captivated by the elegance of language fusion, the mastery of cross-cultural comprehension, and the transformation of algorithms into linguistic ambassadors – a voyage that transcends borders, creating a realm where words are

Mastering Artificial Intelligence and Machine Learning bridges and communication knows no bounds.

Multilingual Magic: Uniting the Linguistic Pantheon

Envision a digital Babel, where algorithms possess the gift of tongues, effortlessly conversing in a multitude of languages. Multilingual applications are the envoys of this linguistic pantheon, transcending barriers to weave a tapestry of global interaction. From translation to sentiment analysis, they harmonize languages, transforming text into a universal symphony.

In the realm of business, multilingual chatbots serve as digital interpreters, facilitating cross-border negotiations. In social media, sentiment analysis algorithms embrace diversity, gauging emotions across languages and cultures. Multilingual search engines become portals to a world of knowledge, transforming queries into cross-lingual journeys.

Cross-Lingual Comprehension: The Unity of Diversity

Imagine a bridge across the chasm of language, where understanding flows freely between tongues. Cross-Lingual applications construct this bridge, fusing linguistic diversity into a tapestry of comprehension. They empower machines to interpret languages, analyze trends, and synthesize information, transcending barriers to create a realm of shared knowledge.

In research, cross-lingual information retrieval becomes a beacon of discovery, enabling scholars to access global knowledge repositories. Sentiment analysis algorithms decipher global opinions, harmonizing cultural expressions into a coherent narrative. Multilingual data fusion transforms dispersed information into a symphony of insight, revealing patterns that span continents.

The Uncharted Territories: Multilingual NLP and Beyond

In the grand theater of Natural Language Processing, Multilingual applications emerge as the virtuosos of linguistic fusion, transcending single languages to shape a global narrative. Multilingual neural machine translation, guided by a single model, becomes the Rosetta Stone of communication, translating with eloquence across diverse tongues. Multilingual Named Entity Recognition becomes a cosmopolitan diplomat, recognizing entities regardless of linguistic attire.

Cross-Lingual embeddings bridge language gaps, enabling algorithms to map semantic landscapes that span cultures. Sentiment analysis algorithms become global barometers of emotion, revealing the heartbeat of humanity in countless languages.

Cross-Cultural Connection: The Promise of Diplomatic Discourse

In the realm of applications, Multilingual and Cross-Lingual tools stand as the diplomats of digital discourse, shaping a world where communication transcends linguistic boundaries. They foster unity in diversity, enabling understanding, and nurturing connections across cultures. Multilingual chatbots become conversation companions that traverse linguistic chasms, creating bridges of dialogue. Cross-Lingual sentiment analysis becomes a cultural empath, deciphering emotions and unifying global voices.

As we navigate this landscape of linguistic diplomacy, we witness the alchemy of language fusion, the mastery of cross-cultural comprehension, and the symphony of global interaction. Multilingual and Cross-Lingual applications are not just algorithms; they are the architects of unity, the envoys of cross-cultural harmony, and the embodiment of communication's universal melody. They become the vessels through which languages interweave, cultures converge, and humanity's diverse voices harmonize into a tapestry of understanding and connection.

CHAPTER 12

AI in Image and Video Analysis

In the realm where pixels dance and images speak, AI in Image and Video Analysis emerges as the conjurer of visual enchantment – the sorcerer that deciphers visual tales, the sculptor that breathes life into pixels. Imagine a world where algorithms unravel the essence of images, capturing emotions and detecting anomalies with a glance, while videos are dissected into cinematic frames of meaning – this is the realm of visual alchemy. As we traverse this enchanted domain, prepare to be captivated by the artistry of image recognition, the wizardry of motion analysis, and the transformation of algorithms into seers of visual narratives – a journey that transcends sight, reshaping the very canvas of visual understanding and weaving a tapestry where data and art converge.

A. Object detection and image segmentation

In the grand gallery of visual perception, where pixels give birth to meaning and images tell stories, Object Detection and Image Segmentation emerge as the virtuoso painters of artificial intelligence – the visionaries that trace the contours of objects, the architects that demarcate boundaries, and the enchanters that grant algorithms the gift of sight. Imagine a canvas where algorithms discern objects in the chaos of pixels and create silhouettes that dance on the edge of recognition – this is the essence of Object Detection and Image Segmentation. As we delve into this realm of visual mastery, prepare to be entranced by the precision of object spotting, the magic of boundary delineation, and the metamorphosis of code into visual artists – a voyage that transcends the mundane, transforming data into the vibrant palette of visual insight and weaving the fabric of a world where algorithms see and interpret with an artist's eye.

Object Detection: Unveiling the Hidden Shapes

Envision an algorithmic detective, equipped with a magnifying glass, combing through a sea of pixels to unveil the hidden shapes of objects. Object Detection is this sleuth, the maestro that identifies and localizes objects within images. It's a symphony of feature extraction and spatial mapping, where pixels transform into meaningful forms.

Object Detection algorithms, whether based on region proposal networks or single-shot detection, wield a virtual magnifying glass that highlights objects' outlines. They decode images, revealing the presence and positions of objects, infusing pixels with semantic significance. From autonomous vehicles navigating streets to security systems spotting intruders, Object Detection is the vigilant sentinel, transforming raw visual data into actionable understanding.

Image Segmentation: The Art of Boundary Carving

Imagine an algorithmic artist wielding a chisel, carving intricate boundaries within images. Image Segmentation is this artisan, the sculptor of visual precision that divides images into coherent segments, each a masterpiece of spatial separation. It's a symphony of pixel grouping, where colors and textures converge to create meaning.

Image Segmentation algorithms, be they based on region-based or pixel-based approaches, analyze textures and intensities to identify distinct regions. They delineate boundaries with finesse, crafting visual puzzles where each piece is a cohesive fragment of the larger mosaic. From medical imaging discerning tumors' contours to satellite imagery mapping urban landscapes, Image Segmentation transforms images into spatial narratives, fostering an understanding that transcends the pixelated veil.

Semantic and Instance Segmentation: Layers of Complexity

Envision an algorithmic architect constructing layers of visual comprehension, akin to transparent overlays that reveal ever-deeper meanings. Semantic Segmentation is this architect, coloring images with a palette of semantic labels, assigning each pixel to a class. It's a symphony of categorization, where pixels metamorphose into meaningful segments.

Instance Segmentation, a more intricate virtuoso, not only paints the semantic canvas but also distinguishes individual instances within the same class. It's a symphony of pixel-level discrimination, where each instance emerges as a distinct brushstroke within the semantic panorama.

Beyond Sight: Applications in a Visual Realm

In the grand theater of applications, Object Detection and Image Segmentation stand as the interpreters of visual narratives. In the realm of autonomous vehicles, Object Detection ensures safety by identifying pedestrians and obstacles. In agriculture, it optimizes crop yield by detecting diseased plants. Image Segmentation, in medical imaging, aids diagnoses by outlining anomalies, while in augmented reality, it overlays virtual objects onto the real world.

In the symphony of AI's artistic expression, Object Detection and Image Segmentation become the brushstrokes that bring meaning to visual data. They uncover objects concealed within pixels, creating silhouettes that capture reality's essence. These algorithms are more than mere tools; they are the visionaries that breathe life into images, deciphering their intricate language and transforming them into windows to a world seen through an algorithmic eye.

B. Video understanding and action recognition

In the captivating realm of moving frames and unfolding narratives, Video Understanding and Action Recognition emerge as the prodigies of artificial intelligence – the auteurs that decode visual epics, the choreographers that dissect motion, and the enchanters that grant algorithms the gift of perceiving time's tapestry. Imagine a theater where algorithms unravel the plotlines of videos and unravel the language of gestures, crafting a symphony of context and motion – this is the essence of Video Understanding and Action Recognition. As we step into this domain of visual cognition, prepare to be entranced by the intricacies of motion analysis, the wizardry of activity inference, and the metamorphosis of algorithms into storytellers of the digital screen – a journey that transcends frames, where data flows as time's river and algorithms become maestros of cinematic comprehension.

Video Understanding: Decoding the Moving Mosaic

Envision an algorithmic connoisseur seated in a theater, interpreting the sequences of frames that flicker before its digital eyes. Video Understanding is this connoisseur, the virtuoso that unravels temporal tales, extracting context and meaning from sequences of images. It's a symphony of spatial and temporal correlations, where pixels metamorphose into stories that unfold with each passing frame.

Video Understanding algorithms are cinematic interpreters, analyzing motion patterns and scene changes. They capture the ebb and flow of movement, deciphering stories that traverse the dimension of time. From surveillance systems monitoring crowd behavior to sports analytics dissecting athletes' strategies, Video Understanding becomes the seer of motion's narrative, transforming raw visual data into a symphony of insight.

Action Recognition: The Choreography of Gesture

Imagine an algorithmic choreographer observing a dance of pixels, attuned to the rhythm of gestures and the language of motion. Action Recognition is this choreographer, the conductor that deciphers human and object movements, translating pixels into steps of meaning. It's a symphony of feature extraction and classification, where visual dynamics become linguistic expression.

Action Recognition algorithms analyze motion's tempo and style, distinguishing activities from a repertoire of gestures. They discern the minutiae of human movement, understanding actions as diverse as running, gesturing, or lifting. From human-computer interaction to surveillance identifying suspicious behaviors, Action Recognition becomes the interpreter of motion, transmuting visual kinetics into a symphony of actionable understanding.

Temporal Understanding: The Symphony of Context

Envision an algorithmic composer orchestrating the symphony of time, where frames blend into a continuum of narrative coherence. Temporal Understanding is this composer, fusing Video Understanding and Action Recognition into a harmonious narrative that transcends the boundaries of individual moments. It's a symphony of context, where sequences unite to unveil stories of interaction, intention, and emotion.

Temporal Understanding algorithms stitch frames into a cohesive fabric, unveiling the subtle nuances of change and progression. They capture the interplay between motion and context, identifying not only what is happening but also the narrative's flow. From analyzing crowd behavior in public spaces to interpreting human intentions in driver assistance systems, Temporal Understanding becomes the guardian of time's secrets, transforming frames into chapters of a visual saga.

Beyond Visual Perception: Applications in Dynamic Realms

In the grand theater of applications, Video Understanding and Action Recognition transcend pixels to become interpreters of dynamic realms. In healthcare, Video Understanding monitors patient movement to aid diagnostics and rehabilitation. In robotics, Action Recognition guides machines to mimic human gestures. In entertainment, Video Understanding fuels content recommendation systems that cater to individual preferences.

As the maestros of video's symphony, Video Understanding and Action Recognition become the interpreters of visual narratives. They read the silent language of motion, recognizing gestures that narrate stories untold. These algorithms are not just observers; they are the auteurs of visual comprehension, deciphering time's enigma and unraveling the dances of pixels, transforming them into tales of interaction, emotion, and life.

C. Generative models for image synthesis

In the realm where pixels play and imagination knows no bounds, Generative Models for Image Synthesis emerge as the modern-day da Vincis of artificial intelligence – the painters of pixels, the architects of visual dreams, and the conjurers that harness algorithms to breathe life into the canvas of the digital world. Imagine an atelier where code and creativity converge, where algorithms wield brushes of data to craft images that evoke emotions, spark wonder, and ignite the flames of artistic innovation – this is the essence of Generative Models for Image Synthesis. As we step into this domain of pixel alchemy, prepare to be mesmerized by the orchestration of latent spaces, the wizardry of adversarial duels, and the metamorphosis of algorithms into digital artists – a journey that transcends reality, where data and imagination intertwine to shape a visual realm that dances to the tune of algorithms' strokes.

Generative Artistry: Unleashing the Latent Potential

Envision an abstract dimension, a realm of latent variables where creativity resides in a dormant state. Generative Models for Image Synthesis are the sculptors of this dimension, molding latent variables into a gallery of visual marvels. It's a symphony of statistical distribution, where the randomness of latent space transmutes into structured artistry.

Variational Autoencoders (VAEs) and Generative Adversarial Networks (GANs) orchestrate this transformation. VAEs traverse the latent space, unlocking its artistic potential and mapping it to images. GANs, on the other hand, engage in an adversarial dance, where a generator learns to mimic reality and a discriminator learns to tell fact from fiction. Together, they imbue pixels with latent whispers, crafting images that defy reality's constraints.

The Dance of Adversarial Duel: GANs as Artistic Pioneers

Imagine an algorithmic duel on the canvas of data, where a generator and a discriminator engage in a ballet of deception and discernment. Generative Adversarial Networks (GANs) are this dueling pair, the pioneers that pit algorithms against each other to birth images of unparalleled authenticity. It's a symphony of equilibrium, where the generator strives to create artful deception while the discriminator evolves to become an unyielding art critic.

The generator learns the language of pixels, crafting images that mirror the dataset's essence. The discriminator hones its discernment, distinguishing the true from the artificial. As they dance this adversarial duet, GANs create images that captivate with realism, transforming algorithmic sparring into an artistic masterpiece.

Conditional Creativity: The Symphony of Controlled Synthesis

Envision an artist's palette where every brushstroke follows a predefined theme. Conditional Generative Models wield this palette, crafting images under specific guidance. It's a symphony of controlled synthesis, where algorithms generate images based on specified conditions, turning data into customizable visual narratives.

Conditional Variational Autoencoders (CVAEs) and Conditional GANs extend the canvas of generative artistry. They allow for controlled exploration of latent space, generating images that conform to desired attributes. From creating art based on text descriptions to generating personalized avatars, conditional generative models transform algorithms into art directors, molding pixels according to predefined themes.

Beyond Reality: Applications in the Visual Realm

In the grand theater of applications, Generative Models for Image Synthesis transcend pixels to become creators of virtual worlds. In fashion, generative models design clothing and accessories. In design, they create architectural marvels and interior spaces. In entertainment, they craft visual effects and generate lifelike characters.

As the architects of visual dreams, Generative Models for Image Synthesis become the brushstrokes of digital artistry. They fuse latent variables and adversarial creativity to birth images that evoke emotions, spark innovation, and challenge the boundaries of reality. These algorithms are more than tools; they are the pioneers of generative art, the maestros of pixel orchestration, and the embodiment of algorithms' potential to shape the visual tapestry of our digital existence.

Part IV

Advanced AI and ML Topics

CHAPTER 13

Bayesian Learning and Probabilistic Graphical Models

In the intricate web of data and the enigma of uncertainty, Bayesian Learning and Probabilistic Graphical Models emerge as the cartographers of probability's terrain – the navigators of uncertainty, the alchemists of inference, and the conjurers that unveil hidden relationships within complex systems. Imagine a realm where algorithms decipher the intricate dance of probabilities, mapping connections between variables and unraveling the secrets of uncertainty – this is the essence of Bayesian Learning and Probabilistic Graphical Models. As we embark on this journey through the labyrinth of uncertainty, prepare to be captivated by the elegance of probabilistic reasoning, the magic of graphical representation, and the metamorphosis of algorithms into interpreters of the unseen – a voyage that transcends data, weaving a tapestry of interconnected probabilities and guiding us through the cryptic realm of statistical insight.

A. Bayesian networks and conditional independence

In the realm of data's intricate dance and uncertainty's shrouded veil, Bayesian Networks emerge as the celestial navigators of probabilistic understanding – the architects of conditional wisdom, the custodians of dependencies, and the artisans that craft a symphony of interconnected probabilities. Imagine a world where data threads weave a tapestry of hidden relationships, and algorithms unveil the orchestration of cause and effect – this is the realm of Bayesian Networks. As we delve into this landscape of probabilistic brilliance, prepare to be entranced by the intricacies of conditional independence, the elegance of graphical representation, and the metamorphosis of algorithms into interpreters of probabilistic destiny – a journey that transcends variables, where data becomes a constellation of insights and algorithms decipher the enigmatic patterns of uncertainty.

Unraveling Dependencies: The Art of Conditional Independence

Envision a realm where events synchronize in a dance of hidden relationships, where the occurrence of one event subtly influences another. Conditional Independence is the torchbearer that illuminates this intricate choreography, the cartographer that deciphers the dependencies hidden within data's folds. It's a symphony of statistical harmony, where variables interplay while maintaining their unique narratives.

Bayesian Networks capture this dance with eloquence. Graphical nodes represent variables, and edges signify dependencies. A node's conditional probability distribution encapsulates the essence of its connection to other nodes. The magic lies in conditional independence, where the knowledge of certain variables renders others independent. It's a symphony of probabilistic autonomy, where data's threads converge and diverge with elegance.

Graphical Elegance: Illuminating Probabilistic Landscapes

Imagine a canvas where data's essence materializes as a constellation of nodes, where connections and dependencies weave an intricate tapestry. Bayesian Networks are the artists that paint this canvas with probabilistic brushstrokes, transforming complex relationships into an elegantly interconnected graph. It's a symphony of visual representation, where data's intricacies transform into a masterpiece of graphical elegance.

Bayesian Networks' graphical form reveals dependencies at a glance. Nodes harmonize variables, and edges become bridges between statistical islands. As dependencies unfold, the network unveils the ripple effect of one variable's influence on another. It's a symphony of graphical insight, where complex probabilistic relationships are transformed into an intuitive landscape of interconnected nodes and edges.

Applications of Wisdom: Navigating Complex Systems

In the grand theater of applications, Bayesian Networks transcend abstraction, becoming the interpreters of complex systems. In healthcare, they diagnose diseases by tracing symptoms' causal pathways. In finance, they analyze market trends by untangling economic variables. In engineering, they optimize processes by revealing interdependent factors.

Bayesian Networks are more than algorithms; they are the compasses that guide us through the sea of uncertainty. They distill probabilistic relationships into graphical form, unveiling the symphony of conditional independence and dependencies that govern our world. These networks are the interpreters of causality's language, the architects of insight, and the embodiment of algorithms' ability to illuminate the hidden connections that underlie the data's surface.

B. Hidden Markov models and dynamic systems

In the symphony of data's evolution and the mysteries of hidden dynamics, Hidden Markov Models (HMMs) emerge as the enigmatic storytellers of probabilistic change – the decipherers of unobserved states, the conjurers of latent transitions, and the architects that illuminate the cryptic dance of underlying systems. Imagine a world where data's rhythm conceals hidden melodies, and algorithms unveil the echoes of unobservable states – this is the realm of Hidden Markov Models. As we embark on this journey through the labyrinth of dynamic insights, prepare to be captivated by the intricacies of latent variables, the magic of state transitions, and the metamorphosis of algorithms into interpreters of concealed narratives – a voyage that transcends observations, weaving a tapestry of hidden patterns and guiding us through the enigmatic realm of dynamic phenomena.

Unseen States: The Artistry of Hidden Markov Models

Envision an orchestral conductor poised to interpret an invisible score – Hidden Markov Models embody this conductor, the maestro that harmonizes observed outcomes with unobserved states. It's a symphony of probabilistic interplay, where states remain hidden, yet their whispers are captured through observable emissions.

Hidden Markov Models craft this symphony by defining states, their transitions, and the probabilities of generating observable outcomes. A symphony's movement becomes a state, while the audible notes it produces are the emissions. Through iterative algorithms like the Baum-Welch method, HMMs learn hidden states and transitions, revealing the unseen narrative woven through data's veil.

Dynamic Transitions: The Dance of Latent Variables

Imagine a choreography of transitions where the steps remain concealed – Hidden Markov Models are the choreographers of this dance, the interpreters that uncover the underlying sequence of events. It's a symphony of latent dynamics, where transitions between states remain obscured, yet their patterns are discerned through observations.

Hidden Markov Models map this dance with mathematical precision. They model state transitions and the probabilities of moving from one latent state to another. These transitions hold the key to deciphering dynamic systems' behavior. In applications like speech recognition, HMMs decode audio phonemes, while in bioinformatics, they unveil genomic sequences' hidden codes.

Learning from Observations: The Alchemy of Inference

Envision an alchemist distilling wisdom from the cauldron of observations – Hidden Markov Models embody this alchemy, the sorcerers that infer unobservable states based on observed emissions. It's a symphony of probabilistic deduction, where observations offer hints to the underlying dynamics.

Hidden Markov Models achieve this magic through the Viterbi algorithm, which deciphers the most likely sequence of hidden states that produced the observable emissions. This process resembles finding the best narrative to match observed events, uncovering the latent story that aligns with data's manifestations.

Applications in Dynamic Realms: Unveiling Enigmatic Systems

In the grand theater of applications, Hidden Markov Models become interpreters of dynamic realms. In speech recognition, they transmute audio waves into linguistic phonemes. In finance, they decode market trends by discerning latent economic states. In neuroscience, they untangle neural firing patterns, revealing unobservable brain dynamics.

Hidden Markov Models are more than algorithms; they are the seers of concealed narratives, the interpreters of latent transitions, and the embodiment of algorithms' power to decipher the hidden layers beneath observable phenomena. These models orchestrate the symphony of dynamic systems, revealing patterns that resonate with the whispers of unobservable variables and illuminating the cryptic dynamics that govern our world.

C. Applications in medical diagnosis and finance

In the realms where lives intertwine with algorithms and fortunes pivot on data's edge, Artificial Intelligence (AI) emerges as the healer of afflictions and the fortune teller of markets – the virtuoso that deciphers medical mysteries, the oracle that navigates financial tides, and the maestro that transforms data into insights that shape lives and destinies. Imagine a world where algorithms lend their intelligence to diagnose diseases with unprecedented accuracy and predict market trends with uncanny foresight – this is the essence of AI's applications in Medical Diagnosis and Finance. As we embark on this dual odyssey through the corridors of health and the pathways of wealth, prepare to be captivated by the precision of medical prognosis, the clairvoyance of market analysis, and the metamorphosis of algorithms into agents of well-being and prosperity – a journey that transcends medical records and financial sheets, weaving a tapestry where data metamorphoses into health-preserving decisions and wealth-maximizing strategies.

Medical Diagnosis: Healing with Algorithmic Insight

Envision a digital clinic where algorithms don the roles of diagnosticians, sifting through medical records with a discerning eye. AI in Medical Diagnosis is this modern-day healer, the virtuoso that analyzes symptoms, deciphers patterns, and offers insights that sharpen medical decisions. It's a symphony of data interpretation, where electronic health records and medical images transform into a landscape of insights.

In applications like medical imaging, AI deciphers X-rays, MRIs, and CT scans, aiding radiologists in spotting anomalies. In diagnostics, algorithms analyze patient data, offering predictive insights into potential illnesses. AI assists in personalized treatment plans, ensuring therapies align with individual biology.

It becomes the stethoscope that listens to data's heartbeat, diagnosing ailments with a precision that empowers healthcare practitioners and transforms patient outcomes.

Finance: Navigating Wealth's Seas with Algorithmic Compass

Imagine an algorithmic navigator aboard a financial vessel, steering through volatile waters with precision and foresight. AI in Finance is this navigator, the sentinel that analyzes market data, identifies trends, and offers strategies that ride the waves of profitability. It's a symphony of data interpretation, where price movements, historical data, and economic indicators converge into a symphony of insights.

In trading, AI analyzes market conditions, executing buy and sell orders with split-second decisions. In risk management, algorithms assess investment portfolios, balancing risk and reward. AI becomes the quant guru, revealing statistical nuances and uncovering arbitrage opportunities. It becomes the compass that guides investors through financial tumult, maximizing gains while minimizing losses.

Parallel Applications: Insights and Fortunes Unveiled

In the grand theater of applications, AI reshapes medical diagnostics and financial strategies, leaving an indelible mark. In medical research, AI sifts through genomics data, identifying genetic markers for diseases. In financial analytics, AI predicts stock prices, shaping investment strategies. Parallelly, AI-driven anomaly detection identifies fraudulent activities both in medical claims and financial transactions.

AI in Medical Diagnosis and Finance doesn't just analyze data; it orchestrates a symphony of insight. It becomes the companion of doctors, enhancing their expertise. It evolves into the strategist for investors, augmenting their decisions. In both domains, AI transcends conventional practices, sculpting a realm where data becomes a catalyst for informed action.

Beyond Algorithms: Healing Lives and Shaping Fortunes

AI's applications in Medical Diagnosis and Finance are not just technological marvels; they are the healers of bodies and architects of prosperity. They decipher medical puzzles, offering glimpses into health's horizons. They navigate financial realms, offering strategies that capitalize on opportunities. These applications are the interpreters of data's wisdom, the guardians of well-being, and the embodiments of algorithms' potential to mend ailments and steer destinies.

CHAPTER 14

Transfer Learning and Model Interpretability

In the realm where knowledge journeys across domains and algorithms yield insights, Transfer Learning and Model Interpretability stand as the pillars of AI's transcendence – the voyagers of knowledge, the architects of understanding, and the conjurers that bridge the gap between data and human comprehension. Imagine a universe where algorithms glean wisdom from one domain and apply it to another, while also allowing us to unravel the intricacies of their decision-making – this is the essence of Transfer Learning and Model Interpretability. As we embark on this dual odyssey, prepare to be captivated by the art of knowledge transfer, the alchemy of model introspection, and the metamorphosis of algorithms into interpretable guides that illuminate the pathways of data's transformation and insights' emergence – a journey that transcends data silos, revealing the seamless flow of wisdom and the emergence of clarity within the intricacies of AI's cognitive landscape.

A. Transfer learning strategies and fine-tuning

In the realm where data's melodies resonate across domains and algorithms harmonize with newfound wisdom, Transfer Learning Strategies and the symphony of Fine-Tuning emerge as the virtuosos of AI's evolution – the maestros of knowledge transfer, the architects of specialization, and the artisans that weave a tapestry of pre-trained expertise and domain-specific finesse. Imagine a world where algorithms seamlessly inherit knowledge from one domain and refine it to excel in another, conducting a symphony of cognitive migration – this is the essence of Transfer Learning Strategies and Fine-Tuning. As we step onto this grand stage of algorithmic evolution, prepare to be captivated by the intricacies of domain adaptation, the magic of parameter refinement, and the metamorphosis of algorithms into polymaths of data, effortlessly transitioning from one expertise to another and striking chords of innovation that reverberate across the landscape of artificial intelligence.

Transfer Learning Strategies: The Art of Cognitive Migration

Envision an algorithmic traveler embarking on a journey from one domain to another, carrying the torch of wisdom to illuminate uncharted territories. Transfer Learning Strategies are this agile traveler, the custodians of cross-domain knowledge that harmonize previously acquired expertise with the demands of a new landscape. It's a symphony of data alignment, where algorithms adapt and evolve, leveraging insights gained in one domain to thrive in another.

Transfer Learning Strategies unfold in various harmonies – domain adaptation, where models are adjusted to the nuances of a new domain; pre-training, where algorithms learn foundational concepts from vast datasets before specializing; and feature extraction, where intermediary layers become bridges between domains. Through these strategies, algorithms become polyglots of data, seamlessly translating their cognitive prowess across the lexicons of different disciplines.

Fine-Tuning: Sculpting Expertise with Precision

Imagine an algorithmic sculptor, chiseling away the rough edges of general knowledge to craft a masterpiece of domain expertise. Fine-Tuning is this sculptor, the artisan that refines parameters, recalibrates weights, and orchestrates a harmonious convergence of knowledge and specialization. It's a symphony of parameter adjustment, where pre-trained models are polished to shine brilliantly in a specific domain.

Fine-Tuning dances with the data's nuances, learning from the specific characteristics of the target domain. It guides the algorithm's evolution, allowing it to retain the foundational wisdom of pre-training while adapting to the intricacies of the new landscape. From medical image diagnosis to natural language translation, Fine-Tuning amplifies the symphony of data's harmonies, transforming a generalist into a virtuoso performer.

Applications: From Knowledge Inheritance to Mastery

In the grand theater of applications, Transfer Learning Strategies and Fine-Tuning take center stage. In computer vision, models pre-trained on large image datasets specialize in medical image analysis, spotting anomalies with unmatched accuracy. In natural language processing, language models pivot their linguistic prowess to translate technical documents with domain-specific fluency. In robotics, algorithms pre-trained for one task evolve to excel in novel environments, performing intricate maneuvers.

These strategies transcend mere algorithms; they are the custodians of knowledge inheritance, the sculptors of expertise, and the architects of innovation. They showcase the dynamic adaptability of AI, seamlessly transferring wisdom and mastering new realms with finesse. Like virtuoso performers, they harmonize inherited knowledge with domain-specific brilliance, enriching the symphony of AI's evolution with resounding notes of cognitive synergy.

B. Explainable AI and model interpretability techniques

In the enigmatic realm where algorithms weave their magic and data's secrets lie veiled, Explainable AI and Model Interpretability emerge as the sages of transparency – the elucidators of hidden decisions, the architects of insights, and the conjurers that unravel the esoteric narratives within the labyrinth of machine learning. Imagine a world where algorithms not only predict but also articulate the reasoning behind their choices, illuminating the darkest corners of the black box – this is the essence of Explainable AI and Model Interpretability. As we embark on this journey through the corridors of algorithmic introspection, prepare to be captivated by the art of unveiling, the craft of feature attribution, and the metamorphosis of algorithms into interpretable companions that decode the symphony of data's transformations and guide us through the intricate maze of AI's cognitive landscape.

Explainable AI: The Key to the Black Box

Envision an AI oracle that not only predicts outcomes but also reveals its thought process, akin to a trail of breadcrumbs leading through the forest of complexity. Explainable AI is this oracle, the interpreter of algorithmic decision-making, bridging the gap between mathematical abstraction and human comprehension. It's a symphony of intelligibility, where predictions come with transparent explanations, transforming complex predictions into coherent narratives.

Explainable AI takes various forms – from rule-based models that map decisions to understandable logic, to surrogate models that mimic the black-box model's behavior. LIME (Local

Interpretable Model-Agnostic Explanations) creates interpretable models to explain predictions, while SHAP (SHapley Additive exPlanations) assigns feature contributions to unveil factors shaping predictions. Through these techniques, Explainable AI peels back the layers of complexity, transforming the inscrutable into the comprehensible.

Feature Attribution: Unmasking the Mosaic of Decisions

Imagine an art historian examining a masterpiece, deciphering each brushstroke's contribution to the grandeur of the painting. Feature Attribution is this historian, the analyst that dissects an algorithm's prediction, attributing the significance of each input feature to the final decision. It's a symphony of feature introspection, where contributions are quantified, and predictions are unraveled.

Feature Attribution techniques take diverse forms – from Gradient-based methods that measure feature impact through derivative computations, to Perturbation-based techniques that evaluate feature variations' influence on predictions. Integrated Gradients method quantifies feature contributions along paths from a baseline to the input. In ensemble methods like Random Forest, feature importance scores offer insights into variables shaping predictions.

Applications: From Insights to Ethical Accountability

In the grand theater of applications, Explainable AI and Model Interpretability assume pivotal roles. In healthcare, they elucidate disease diagnoses, articulating the reasons behind predictions. In finance, they demystify credit scoring, revealing the factors influencing lending decisions. In autonomous vehicles, they provide clarity on obstacle avoidance, ensuring the rationale behind critical choices.

These techniques are not just algorithmic tools; they are the guides that navigate us through AI's black box, revealing the thought process behind predictions and fostering trust. They empower users to make informed decisions, allowing practitioners to catch and correct biases or unintended consequences. More than interpreters, they are the conduits of ethical accountability, bridging the chasm between algorithms and human values.

Beyond the Veil: Enlightening Insights and Ethical Empowerment

Explainable AI and Model Interpretability are not mere add-ons; they are the ambassadors of AI's understanding. They unravel the tapestry of predictions, demystifying the enigma of black-box models. They empower us to question, understand, and validate algorithmic decisions. These techniques transform AI from an oracle to a collaborator, enriching the dialogue between data and human insight, and in the process, illuminate the intricate pathways of AI's cognition with the guiding light of transparency.

C. Addressing bias and fairness in AI systems

In the realm where algorithms shape decisions and data's echoes resonate through AI's corridors, addressing bias and fairness emerges as the ethical compass guiding the evolution of artificial intelligence – the guardian against discrimination, the architect of inclusivity, and the sentinel that ensures algorithms mirror the ideals of a just society. Imagine a world where algorithms not only optimize accuracy but also champion fairness, where data's fingerprints are cleansed of bias – this is the essence of addressing bias and fairness in AI systems. As we embark on this journey through the labyrinth of ethical imperative, prepare to be captivated by the intricacies of algorithmic responsibility, the art of data curation, and the metamorphosis of AI systems into instruments that foster a world where data's symphony resonates harmoniously, uninfluenced by the distortions of prejudice.

The Unseen Distortions: The Need to Address Bias

Envision an artist's canvas subtly shaded by preconceptions, where data's hues are tinged with bias, and algorithms perpetuate social inequalities. Addressing bias and fairness is the restorer of this canvas, the artisan that seeks to cleanse data's palette, ensuring that algorithms yield outcomes unmarred by discrimination. It's a symphony of ethical scrutiny, where data's spectrum is purified, and algorithms are scrutinized for potential bias.

Addressing bias requires a multi-faceted approach. From data collection to model deployment, every step is examined. Data is curated with vigilance, biased samples are rectified, and underrepresented voices are amplified. Algorithmic transparency is embraced, allowing stakeholders to understand how decisions are made. Techniques like re-weighting, re-sampling, and adversarial debiasing are wielded, recalibrating the scales of fairness.

Fairness as a North Star: Pioneering Ethical Algorithms

Imagine an AI compass that not only points to accurate predictions but also guides us toward equitable outcomes, a compass that transcends data's prejudices. Fairness is this compass, the lodestar that ensures AI systems uphold values of justice and inclusivity. It's a symphony of moral navigation, where algorithms are trained to heed the call of fairness, considering the impact of decisions across diverse demographics.

Fairness is achieved through algorithmic audits that assess models for disparate impacts. It involves defining fairness criteria, like demographic parity or equal opportunity, and embedding them into algorithms' training objectives. Techniques like adversarial training strive to reduce disparate treatment of different groups. The aim is to create AI systems that transcend biases, acting as instruments of empowerment for every individual they touch.

Applications: From Equitable Lending to Inclusive Healthcare

In the grand theater of applications, addressing bias and fairness becomes a transformative force. In lending, algorithms ensure that credit decisions are based on financial merit, not demographic attributes. In healthcare, they mitigate disparities in disease diagnosis and treatment recommendations. In criminal justice, they minimize racial bias in risk assessments, fostering more equitable decisions.

These efforts extend beyond algorithms; they are the guardians of ethical AI, the architects of societal progress, and the embodiment of algorithms' potential to harmonize data's symphony. They champion inclusivity, tempering AI's power with ethical responsibility. These techniques go beyond technology; they are the vanguards of change, redefining the landscape of AI and nurturing a world where algorithms mirror the ethos of a just and equitable society.

CHAPTER 15

Deep Reinforcement Learning

In the realm where algorithms evolve into cognitive mavericks, navigating landscapes through trial, error, and unprecedented learning, Deep Reinforcement Learning emerges as the visionary explorer of artificial intelligence – the captain of decision-making ships, the architect of learning through experience, and the conjurer that pushes the boundaries of machine learning to the abyss of unparalleled accomplishments. Imagine a universe where algorithms, fueled by data and guided by rewards, master intricate tasks and embrace complex environments, akin to a symphony of intelligence in action – this is the essence of Deep Reinforcement Learning. As we embark on this odyssey through the ocean of reinforcement, prepare to be captivated by the intricate dance of actions and consequences, the marvel of policy optimization, and the metamorphosis of algorithms into agents of adaptive prowess that transcend mere data manipulation, ushering in an era of AI that learns, adapts, and triumphs with the grace of a maestro at its zenith.

A. Deep Q-Networks (DQN) and policy gradients

In the labyrinth of decision-making and the symphony of

actions and rewards, Deep Q-Networks (DQNs) and Policy Gradients emerge as the architects of AI's evolutionary plunge – the pioneers of value-driven learning, the maestros of policy optimization, and the conjurers that sculpt algorithms into virtuosos of adaptive prowess. Imagine a realm where algorithms don the mantle of experience, charting territories of decision landscapes, and policies are sculpted into masterpieces of action – this is the essence of Deep Q-Networks and Policy Gradients. As we venture into the depths of AI's cognitive abyss, prepare to be captivated by the harmonious interplay of exploration and exploitation, the elegance of action-value estimation, and the metamorphosis of algorithms into agents that not only learn but orchestrate a symphony of actions that yield triumph in the grand theater of decision-making.

Deep Q-Networks (DQNs): The Odyssey of Value-driven Learning

Envision an algorithmic voyager charting a course through a sea of possible actions, with each wave revealing insights and rewards. Deep Q-Networks are this navigator, the trailblazer that balances exploration and exploitation, discerning the optimal path through a thicket of choices. It's a symphony of value estimation, where algorithms learn to assess the potential of actions and optimize decisions based on anticipated rewards.

DQNs achieve this feat through a neural network architecture that approximates the Q-value, a metric that quantifies the expected cumulative reward for taking a specific action in a given state. With the convergence of experience replay and target networks, DQNs strike a harmonious balance between revisiting past actions and striving for novel exploration. The result is an algorithmic marvel that transcends mere decision-making, evolving into an orchestration of calculated actions, each a step towards mastery.

Policy Gradients: The Artistry of Policy Optimization

Imagine an algorithmic artist refining brushstrokes to create a masterpiece of decision-making. Policy Gradients are this artist, the sculptor that shapes policies into elegantly orchestrated sequences of actions. It's a symphony of parameter adjustments, where algorithms learn to iteratively refine policies, optimizing them to maximize cumulative rewards.

Policy Gradients waltz through a landscape of gradients, adjusting policy parameters to enhance the likelihood of actions that yield higher rewards. By embracing the magic of gradient descent, algorithms navigate the nuances of action sequences, adapting policies to traverse landscapes of decision scenarios. In this ballet of optimization, policies evolve into crescendos of actions, each note an embodiment of strategic mastery.

Applications: From Gaming Triumphs to Robotic Marvels

In the grand theater of applications, Deep Q-Networks and Policy Gradients command the stage. In gaming, DQNs conquer Atari classics, mastering complex strategies through relentless exploration. In robotics, Policy Gradients orchestrate the choreography of robot movements, enabling them to navigate intricate environments and perform precise tasks.

These techniques are more than just algorithms; they are the architects of adaptive agents, the conductors of cognitive symphonies, and the embodiment of AI's potential to learn and triumph. They empower algorithms to not only predict but to act, guiding decision landscapes with precision and orchestrating a harmonious interplay of choices and rewards. These methods revolutionize AI's potential, propelling it into the echelons of decision-making mastery, where actions are no longer just data points but transformative elements in the grand saga of AI's evolution.

B. Continuous action spaces and actor-critic methods

In the realm where algorithms morph into virtuosos of fluid action and decisions flow like the strokes of a maestro's brush, Continuous Action Spaces and Actor-Critic methods emerge as the architects of AI's prowess in the symphony of dynamic decision-making – the conductors of seamless motion, the interpreters of value-driven guidance, and the conjurers that transform algorithms into artists of continuous action. Imagine a world where AI not only navigates complex environments but does so with finesse, akin to a dance of intellect in perpetual motion – this is the essence of Continuous Action Spaces and Actor-Critic methods. As we embark on this journey through the landscapes of dynamic choices, prepare to be captivated by the elegance of fluid decision-making, the harmony of dual perspectives, and the metamorphosis of algorithms into agents that choreograph a seamless ballet of action within the canvas of AI's cognitive evolution.

Continuous Action Spaces: The Ballet of Infinite Choice

Envision an algorithmic dancer on a stage where every move is a nuanced expression, where actions are no longer discrete steps but a continuum of possibilities. Continuous Action Spaces are this dancer, the embodiment of graceful transitions in decision landscapes. It's a symphony of infinite choices, where algorithms sway through a spectrum of actions, expressing their intent with exquisite subtlety.

Continuous Action Spaces embrace a spectrum of actions – be it steering a self-driving car, manipulating robotic arms, or orchestrating financial trades. Algorithms navigate this realm with the finesse of a maestro, selecting actions not from a fixed set but from a seamless range. The result is an algorithmic marvel that transcends the rigidity of step-wise decisions, flowing through the space of possibilities like a river of cognitive fluidity.

Actor-Critic Methods: The Duo of Wisdom and Guidance

Imagine a theatrical production with two protagonists – one assessing the drama, the other fine-tuning performances to perfection. Actor-Critic methods are this duo, the symbiotic relationship of wisdom and guidance that navigates the realm of continuous action. It's a symphony of dynamic learning, where an actor explores actions, and a critic evaluates their value, crafting a harmonious interplay of exploration and refinement.

Actor-Critic methods unfold in harmony – the actor, often a policy network, explores action space, testing the waters of possibility. The critic, a value network, observes the actor's performance and assesses its worth, providing constructive feedback to enhance decision-making. Through iterations of exploration and evaluation, Actor-Critic methods sculpt algorithms into connoisseurs of continuous action, mastering the art of fluid choices.

Applications: From Robotic Precision to Financial Finesse

In the grand theater of applications, Continuous Action Spaces and Actor-Critic methods take center stage. In robotics, algorithms manipulate objects with dexterity, performing intricate tasks that demand fluid motion. In finance, they navigate the tumultuous waters of trading, optimizing investment decisions with a grace that mirrors the elegance of continuous action.

These methods are more than just algorithms; they are the choreographers of AI's dance through dynamic landscapes, the architects of continuous excellence, and the embodiment of algorithms' potential to embrace fluidity in decision-making. They empower AI to not only adapt but to flow, guiding action seamlessly through a realm of infinite possibilities. These techniques transcend conventional algorithms, elevating AI to a state of perpetual motion, where decisions are no longer mere choices but the exquisite brushstrokes of cognitive artistry.

C. Real-world applications in robotics and gaming

In the realms where innovation meets mechanics and imagination melds with digital landscapes, real-world applications in robotics and the expanse of gaming emerge as the heralds of transformative experiences – the architects of tangible advancements, the sorcerers of virtual realms, and the conjurers that bind the physical and the digital into an intricate tapestry of human ingenuity. Imagine a world where machines execute intricate tasks with precision, where virtual worlds offer adventures unbound by reality – this is the essence of real-world applications in robotics and the captivating saga of gaming. As we embark on this dual odyssey, prepare to be captivated by the symphony of mechanical finesse, the enchantment of digital narrative, and the metamorphosis of technology into agents of productivity and leisure, painting the canvas of existence with strokes of invention and leisure.

Robotics: Pioneering the Frontier of Mechanical Marvels

Envision a realm where machines don the mantle of collaborators, performing tasks that extend the boundaries of human capability. Real-world applications in robotics are these pioneers, the architects of automation that weave innovation into tangible solutions, from manufacturing to healthcare. It's a symphony of mechanical finesse, where robots mimic human precision, navigating complex environments, and executing tasks with unwavering accuracy.

In manufacturing, robotic arms assemble intricate components, creating products with unrivaled precision and efficiency. In healthcare, robots assist surgeons, enhancing procedures with a surgeon's precision and a machine's steadiness. In logistics, autonomous drones navigate terrain to deliver packages, revolutionizing supply chains. These applications are not just mechanical marvels; they are the harbingers of efficiency, amplifying human capabilities and transforming industries with an orchestration of mechanics and technology.

Gaming: Crafting Epic Narratives in Digital Realms

Imagine a universe where players traverse uncharted territories, embark on quests, and sculpt their destinies in the crucible of virtual worlds. Gaming is this storyteller, the realm where narratives are scripted and adventures are scripted anew. Real-world applications in gaming are the architects of these digital odysseys, the conjurers that transport players to alternate realities, crafting experiences that ignite the imagination.

In video games, realistic graphics and physics engines bring worlds to life, immersing players in realms that blur the lines between fiction and reality. In augmented reality (AR) and virtual reality (VR), gaming extends beyond screens, enveloping players in interactive experiences that transcend dimensions. Serious games leverage the power of play for educational purposes, revolutionizing learning through engagement. Gaming is more than entertainment; it's an artistry of technology that engenders creativity, exploration, and shared experiences in digital landscapes.

Parallel Journeys: From Physical Precision to Digital Epics

In the grand tapestry of technological evolution, real-world applications in robotics and gaming walk parallel paths, enriching human existence in diverse dimensions. While robotics empower industries with mechanical mastery, gaming fuels imaginations with digital narratives. They share a common thread of innovation, transforming the mundane into the extraordinary, and the virtual into the visceral.

As robotics deftly maneuver through complex tasks, they pave the way for more efficient manufacturing, personalized healthcare, and autonomous exploration. Meanwhile, gaming captivates minds with interactive narratives, fostering creativity, problem-solving, and social connection. These applications are more than mere technologies; they are the conduits of progress and delight, enhancing the human experience in realms both tangible and virtual.

Bridging Realms: The Confluence of Innovation and Adventure

Real-world applications in robotics and the vast landscapes of gaming are the tapestry weaved by human ingenuity. They celebrate the marvels of technology, from the intricacies of mechanical precision to the expanses of digital imagination. These applications converge at the crossroads of productivity and leisure, empowering industries and enlivening imaginations, each a testament to the symphony of innovation that shapes our ever-evolving world.

CHAPTER 16

AI Ethics and Responsible AI

In the ever-expanding universe of artificial intelligence, where algorithms wield the power of cognition, AI Ethics and Responsible AI emerge as the guiding stars – the custodians of moral integrity, the architects of accountability, and the conjurers that weave a fabric of technology that upholds humanity's values. Imagine a world where machines not only compute but also uphold ethical imperatives, where algorithms are bound by principles that safeguard human dignity – this is the essence of AI Ethics and Responsible AI. As we embark on this cosmic voyage through the realms of technological ethics, prepare to be captivated by the intricacies of algorithmic virtue, the narrative of conscientious AI, and the metamorphosis of algorithms into guardians that shepherd innovation with the grace of moral enlightenment, illuminating the pathways of progress with an unwavering commitment to the greater good.

A. Ethical considerations in AI development

In the crucible of AI development, where algorithms evolve and data yields insights, ethical considerations emerge as the architects of AI's moral integrity – the sculptors of digital virtue, the guardians of societal well-being, and the conjurers that imbue lines of code with the ethos of human values. Imagine a world where algorithms not only optimize efficiency but also champion fairness, where data-driven decisions uphold human dignity – this is the essence of ethical considerations in AI development. As we embark on this odyssey through the labyrinth of AI's ethical landscape, prepare to be captivated by the intricacies of bias mitigation, the symphony of transparency, and the metamorphosis of technology into instruments that echo the aspirations of a just and humane society, forging innovation that harmonizes with the symphony of human values.

The Dilemma of Bias: Pioneering Fairness in Algorithmic Design

Envision an algorithmic arena where decisions echo the echoes of data's past, where hidden biases lurk within the lines of code. Ethical considerations in AI development are the liberators of fairness, the artisans that cleanse data's canvas, ensuring algorithms remain untainted by prejudice. It's a symphony of equitable representation, where diversity becomes a cornerstone of algorithmic design, and the echoes of underrepresented voices resonate through technology's evolution.

Ethical considerations combat bias through techniques like data preprocessing, where imbalances are rectified, and sampling methods ensure equitable representation. Algorithmic audits scrutinize decisions for discriminatory impact, revealing biases hidden beneath the surface. With each iteration, algorithms evolve, transforming into beacons of fairness that champion diversity and challenge the status quo.

Transparency as the Luminary: Unveiling the Black Box

Imagine an algorithmic oracle that not only provides answers but also explains its reasoning, offering a window into the cognitive labyrinth of data-driven decisions. Ethical considerations in AI development are the illuminators of transparency, the sages that demystify the black box, enabling users to understand how and why algorithms make choices. It's a symphony of interpretability, where decisions become narratives, and accountability is woven into the fabric of code.

Transparency mechanisms, from explainable AI techniques to algorithmic audits, pull back the curtain on decision-making processes. Regulatory frameworks demand algorithmic accountability, forcing developers to open the doors of the black box and shed light on its inner workings. With transparency as the guiding star, algorithms transcend obscurity, becoming tools of empowerment rather than enigmas of confusion.

Beyond Technology: The Nexus of Innovation and Responsibility

In the grand theater of AI development, ethical considerations take center stage, illuminating the path to a future where technology and humanity coexist harmoniously. These considerations are not just constraints; they are the architects of innovation with a moral compass, steering algorithms toward a course that aligns with human values. They transcend code, fostering conversations on the impact of AI on society, advocating for policies that ensure technology serves humanity's greater good.

Ethical considerations in AI development redefine progress, shifting the focus from mere technological advancement to responsible innovation. They empower developers to create algorithms that uplift, rather than divide. These considerations shape a narrative where algorithms are not just tools, but responsible agents that weave a symphony of progress, ethics, and humanity, transforming AI into a force that amplifies our collective aspirations.

B. Fairness, transparency, and accountability in AI systems

In the cosmos of artificial intelligence, where algorithms evolve and data fuels the dance of cognition, fairness, transparency, and accountability emerge as the pillars of ethical ascendancy – the guardians of equitable outcomes, the torchbearers of algorithmic integrity, and the conjurers that unveil the moral dimensions of AI's tapestry. Imagine a world where algorithms not only predict but also uphold justice, where data-driven decisions are as transparent as a crystal-clear stream – this is the essence of fairness, transparency, and accountability in AI systems. As we embark on this voyage through the ethical universe of AI, prepare to be captivated by the symphony of balanced representation, the art of algorithmic illumination, and the metamorphosis of technology into agents that not only optimize but also align with the harmony of human values, fostering an era of AI that resonates with the symphony of ethical enlightenment.

Fairness: The Pinnacle of Equitable Algorithms

Envision an algorithmic court where decisions carry the weight of societal implications, where biases distort the scales of justice. Fairness is the compass of this court, the herald of unbiased equilibrium that safeguards against discrimination. It's a symphony of balanced representation, where algorithms champion inclusivity, leveling the playing field and ensuring decisions reflect the mosaic of human diversity.

Fairness techniques counteract biases that emerge from skewed data by recalibrating algorithms. Through re-weighting, re-sampling, and adversarial training, algorithms learn to be blind to attributes irrelevant to decision-making. They embrace fairness metrics, like equal opportunity or demographic parity, guiding their evolution towards unbiased predictions. In this orchestration of equity, algorithms transcend mere computation, becoming agents of social progress that uphold the integrity of justice.

Transparency: The Beacon of Algorithmic Illumination

Imagine an algorithmic gallery where the strokes of data create portraits of decisions, both beautiful and enigmatic. Transparency is the artist's palette, the brush that unveils the decision-making process, offering a window into the cognitive labyrinth. It's a symphony of illumination, where algorithms are not enigmatic black boxes but narratives that unfold with clarity and accountability.

Transparency mechanisms, from explainable AI techniques to algorithmic audits, decode the decisions rendered by algorithms. They reveal the factors influencing predictions, exposing the influence of data and features. Algorithmic accountability becomes woven into the fabric of technology, empowering users to question and validate decisions. With transparency as the guiding star, algorithms transcend opacity, becoming instruments of empowerment that grant insight into their cognitive operations.

Accountability: The Keystone of Ethical AI

In the grand theater of AI systems, where algorithms shape lives and influence outcomes, accountability takes center stage as the conductor of ethical orchestration. It's a symphony of responsibility, where developers and deployers are entrusted with the duty to ensure algorithms' decisions align with societal values and norms. Accountability is the bridge that spans the chasm between innovation and ethical responsibility.

Accountability frameworks demand that AI developers adhere to ethical guidelines, scrutinize algorithms for discriminatory impact, and design safeguards against unintended consequences. Regulatory bodies set the stage for responsible AI deployment, reinforcing the notion that technological advancement must harmonize with ethical principles. In this narrative, accountability extends beyond code, fostering a dialogue where the technology's impact on society is carefully considered, advocating for a future where AI systems uphold human values.

Confluence of Ethical Symphonies: AI as an Instrument of Harmony

Fairness, transparency, and accountability are not just ethical virtues; they are the keystones of AI's moral compass. These considerations harmonize technology's evolution with human values, ensuring that algorithms contribute to a world that is equitable, transparent, and responsible. Together, they form a triumvirate that transcends binary code, fostering a symphony of AI systems that resonate with the ethos of ethical enlightenment. As we navigate the uncharted frontiers of AI's ethical cosmos, let fairness, transparency, and accountability guide us like constellations, illuminating the path to a future where algorithms and humanity coalesce in a harmonious symphony of progress and integrity.

C. Social implications and challenges of AI adoption

In the grand theater of technological evolution, where algorithms dance with data and innovation paints a new dawn, the adoption of Artificial Intelligence (AI) emerges as the symphony of societal transformation – the conductor of efficiency, the maestro of advancement, and the conjurer that heralds a renaissance of human ingenuity. However, within this crescendo of progress, lie shadows of complexity and challenges that cast a profound impact on our social fabric. As we embark on this contemplative odyssey through the implications and challenges of AI adoption, prepare to be captivated by the intricate dance of human-machine coexistence, the crescendo of ethical considerations, and the metamorphosis of societies in the forge of technological evolution.

A Symphony of Coexistence: The Dance of Human-Machine Symbiosis

Imagine a world where algorithms augment human capabilities, where AI seamlessly integrates into our daily lives, assisting in decision-making and streamlining tasks. The adoption of AI is this symphony of coexistence, the harmonious convergence of man and machine. It's a tapestry where algorithms amplify our cognitive prowess, enabling us to tackle challenges of unprecedented complexity, and fostering collaboration that extends beyond conventional boundaries.

AI-driven automation transforms industries, enhancing productivity and unleashing innovation. In healthcare, AI diagnoses diseases with accuracy, augmenting medical practitioners' expertise. In transportation, self-driving cars navigate roads, redefining mobility paradigms. Yet, amidst this harmonious dance, the challenges of preserving human agency, ensuring job stability, and redefining education to cater to AI-augmented skills become the overture of societal transformation.

Ethical Crescendo: The Dilemmas of Algorithmic Conscience

Envision a world where algorithms wield decision-making power, where ethical dilemmas and moral considerations intertwine with lines of code. The adoption of AI is this crescendo of ethical introspection, demanding that the symphony of innovation harmonize with principles that uphold human values. It's an ensemble where algorithms are entrusted with ethical accountability, and humanity grapples with the ramifications of algorithmic judgments.

AI ethics confronts us with profound questions – how do we ensure fairness when algorithms make critical decisions? How do we preserve privacy in an era of data-driven insights? As AI penetrates our lives, the responsibility to imbue algorithms with ethical conscience amplifies. Striking the balance between progress and ethical considerations becomes a fundamental movement in the societal score, orchestrating an enduring melody of AI adoption that echoes with the harmonies of moral introspection.

Reshaping Societal Arrangements: The Dance of Labor and Disruption

In the grand narrative of AI adoption, economic and labor landscapes become arenas of transformation. The adoption of AI is a choreography of labor reimagined, where tasks susceptible to automation are reshaped, and new avenues of work emerge. It's a ballet where the symphony of employment is intertwined with the rhythm of technology's evolution, posing both opportunities and challenges.

AI-driven automation streamlines operations, enhancing efficiency and precision. Yet, it also sparks concerns of job displacement and the urgency of upskilling the workforce for AI-centric roles. Societies must confront the melody of equitable labor transitions, ensuring that the crescendo of innovation does not leave marginalized communities behind. The challenge lies in orchestrating a harmonious cadence where AI adoption is a bridge to prosperity, fostering opportunities that resonate with inclusivity and economic balance.

The Overture of Inclusivity: Composing the Melody of Access and Bias

In the symphony of AI adoption, access to technology becomes a pivotal overture, delineating the boundaries of digital inclusion. The adoption of AI is the composition of digital democracy, demanding that the melody of innovation reaches all corners of society, transcending barriers of geography, income, and education. It's a score where technology bridges divides, empowering marginalized communities and amplifying their voices.

AI-driven tools can perpetuate biases present in data, casting shadows of discrimination in algorithmic decisions. The challenge lies in orchestrating a symphony where inclusivity harmonizes with unbiased technology. Striving for equitable access to AI and mitigating bias requires deliberate actions – from democratizing AI education to rigorously auditing algorithms for fairness. The societal rhythm must resonate with a commitment to creating technology that reverberates with equal opportunity and justice.

Harmonizing the Future: The Composition of Collective Responsibility

In the grand opus of AI adoption, the implications and challenges form the dynamic notes that shape our societal sonata. Just as a symphony is a collective masterpiece, the harmonization of AI's impact on society is a shared endeavor. The future crescendo of AI adoption must be composed with collective responsibility, where governments, industry leaders, researchers, and citizens collaboratively orchestrate a symphony that resonates with human values.

The implications of AI adoption are profound and multifaceted, spanning domains of ethics, labor, accessibility, and societal transformation. Addressing these challenges is not a solo endeavor; it is the composition of a collaborative symphony that resonates with the aspirations of a harmonious technological evolution. As societies navigate the complexities and embrace the opportunities of AI adoption, the melody of progress must harmonize with the rhythms of compassion, equity, and responsible innovation, crafting a composition that reverberates through time as a testament to human ingenuity and resilience.

Part V

AI and ML Applications

CHAPTER 17

AI in Healthcare and Biomedical Sciences

In the realm where innovation melds with compassion, where algorithms don the mantle of healers, and data dances with the rhythm of life, AI in Healthcare and Biomedical Sciences emerges as the symphony of a transformative era – the alchemists of medical discovery, the guardians of precision diagnosis, and the conjurers that weave a tapestry of health and hope. Imagine a world where machines not only compute but also mend, where algorithms dissect the intricacies of diseases, and data-driven decisions illuminate the path to well-being – this is the essence of AI in Healthcare and Biomedical Sciences. As we embark on this profound odyssey through the corridors of medical marvels, prepare to be captivated by the symphony of early disease detection, the art of personalized treatment, and the metamorphosis of technology into a benevolent force that redefines the landscape of healing, painting the canvas of human existence with strokes of innovation and vitality.

A. Medical image analysis and diagnosis

In the realm where pixels become brushstrokes of insight and images are transformed into windows to the body's secrets, medical image analysis and diagnosis emerge as the virtuosos of modern medicine – the interpreters of visual narratives, the architects of early detection, and the conjurers that unlock the enigma of human health. Imagine a world where pixels not only form pictures but also hold the key to unraveling diseases, where algorithms dissect visual cues with surgical precision, and data-driven interpretations carve pathways to recovery – this is the essence of medical image analysis and diagnosis. As we embark on this captivating voyage through the realm of visual exploration in medicine, prepare to be captivated by the symphony of digital artistry, the precision of pattern recognition, and the metamorphosis of images into diagnostic revelations that shape the contours of patient care and well-being.

A Palette of Pixels: The Artistry of Medical Image Analysis

Envision a canvas where X-rays, MRI scans, and microscopic slides compose an intricate mosaic of the body's inner landscapes. Medical image analysis is the palette that transforms these images into diagnostic masterpieces, the brushstrokes of algorithms that decode visual intricacies invisible to the human eye. It's a symphony of digital artistry, where patterns hidden within pixels hold the secrets to diseases, waiting to be unveiled.

Through techniques like image segmentation, algorithms dissect complex visuals, isolating regions of interest with precision. Classification algorithms differentiate between benign and malignant anomalies, guiding clinicians in their diagnostic journey. In this orchestration of pixels and patterns, medical image analysis transcends mere interpretation, becoming an artistic collaboration between technology and human expertise.

The Symphony of Detection: Early Insight into Disease

Imagine a score where images whisper tales of disease at their nascent stages, where algorithms orchestrate the symphony of early detection. Medical image analysis is the conductor of this symphony, the maestro that deciphers subtle visual cues, flagging anomalies long before symptoms manifest. It's a composition of anticipatory precision, where insights gleaned from pixels become the melodies of timely intervention.

Screening mammograms detect breast cancer, ushering in treatment at an early, curable phase. Brain scans unveil the telltale signs of neurological disorders, empowering clinicians to initiate interventions that preserve cognitive health. Early detection becomes a beacon of hope, and medical image analysis stands as its torchbearer, orchestrating the movement towards preventive care.

Beyond the Visual Veil: Unraveling Complexity and Multimodal Insights

In the grand tapestry of medical image analysis, the canvas

extends beyond single images, embracing the symphony of multimodal data. Imagine a narrative where images merge with patient histories, genetic data, and clinical records, harmonizing insights into a comprehensive diagnosis. Medical image analysis is the conductor of this narrative, weaving a tapestry of holistic understanding.

Fusion algorithms amalgamate information from diverse sources, amplifying the diagnostic power of medical images. Integrating genetic data with radiological images unveils personalized treatment pathways, transforming medicine into a bespoke symphony of care. The challenge lies in harmonizing these complex narratives, ensuring that the ensemble of insights paints a cohesive picture that guides clinical decisions.

Empowering Clinicians: Collaborative Interpretation and Beyond

In the symphony of medical image analysis, clinicians wield batons of expertise, collaborating with algorithms to create harmonious diagnostic symphonies. Medical image analysis is the collaborator, the orchestrator that offers insights and augments human interpretation, fostering a synergy that elevates patient care. It's a composition of collaboration, where technology empowers clinicians to make informed decisions that resonate with accuracy and compassion.

Image-based quantification algorithms measure disease

progression, enabling clinicians to monitor treatments' efficacy. Surgical planning algorithms visualize intricate anatomical structures, guiding surgeons in precision procedures. Medical image analysis becomes the ally that enhances clinical prowess, amplifying the impact of human expertise through algorithmic insights.

The Unveiling of Insights: Art, Science, and Healing Converged

In the grand tapestry of medical image analysis and diagnosis, pixels, patterns, and expertise converge in a symphony of healing. This symphony resonates with precision and compassion, shaping patient care and redefining medical narratives. Just as an artist breathes life into a canvas, medical image analysis breathes life into images, transforming them into instruments of diagnosis and beacons of hope.

This transformative journey reveals that medical image analysis is not merely an algorithmic endeavor; it's a narrative of art and science intertwined, a melody of pixels that whispers tales of healing. As technology and human expertise coalesce, the symphony of medical image analysis and diagnosis becomes a testament to the boundless potential of innovation and compassion, painting a vibrant portrait of a future where pixels and patterns weave a tapestry of well-being.

B. Drug discovery and personalized medicine

In the crucible where molecules collide with innovation, where data intertwines with human biology, drug discovery and personalized medicine emerge as the alchemists of modern healthcare – the architects of tailored treatments, the conjurers of molecular marvels, and the custodians of individual well-being. Imagine a world where molecules are not just compounds, but keys to unlocking health, where algorithms dissect genetic blueprints to craft bespoke therapies – this is the essence of drug discovery and personalized medicine. As we embark on this exhilarating expedition through the realm of molecular ingenuity, prepare to be captivated by the symphony of precision therapies, the intricacies of molecular design, and the metamorphosis of molecules into agents of healing, shaping the contours of medical science and igniting a renaissance of individualized care.

The Quest for Miracle Molecules: Pioneering Drug Discovery

Envision a laboratory where molecules are not just compounds, but potential cures waiting to be unveiled. Drug discovery is the quest for these miracle molecules, the artisans that sculpt compounds with the power to combat diseases and alleviate suffering. It's a symphony of molecular design, where algorithms and scientists collaborate to forge new therapies that resonate with precision and efficacy.

In silico drug design techniques leverage computational power to predict the interaction between molecules and targets. Virtual screening algorithms sift through vast chemical libraries, identifying molecules with therapeutic potential. As molecules evolve from chemical sketches to candidates, the symphony of drug discovery conducts a harmonious dance between technology and chemistry, unearthing solutions to medical challenges once deemed insurmountable.

Molecular Navigators: Personalized Medicine's Odyssey

Imagine a landscape where treatments are not prescribed based on generalities, but on the intricacies of individual genetics. Personalized medicine is this odyssey, the navigators that decode genetic maps to craft treatments tailored to each patient's unique molecular makeup. It's a symphony of molecular insights, where genetic data unfurls the narrative of a person's health, guiding interventions with pinpoint accuracy.

Genetic testing algorithms analyze DNA sequences, unveiling genetic mutations and markers that influence disease susceptibility. Pharmacogenomics algorithms decipher how a person's genetic code impacts their response to medications, steering clinicians towards therapies that are effective and safe. The symphony of personalized medicine reverberates with individualized care, harmonizing medical interventions with the rhythm of genetics.

Beyond One-Size-Fits-All: The Precision Paradigm Shift

In the grand narrative of medical progress, drug discovery and personalized medicine converge, heralding a paradigm shift from one-size-fits-all treatments to precision therapies. Imagine a landscape where medications are not just prescriptions, but harmonious chords that resonate with each patient's biology. This is the symphony of precision medicine, where molecules and genetics harmonize to create treatments attuned to individual needs.

Precision medicine algorithms integrate molecular insights with clinical data, forging a holistic understanding of a patient's health. This confluence guides the development of therapies that target diseases at their molecular roots, minimizing side effects and maximizing efficacy. The challenge lies in orchestrating this intricate ensemble of data, algorithms, and patient care, ensuring that precision medicine becomes a harmonious symphony of healing.

The Healing Score: The Patient as a Melody

In the symphony of drug discovery and personalized medicine, the patient is not just a recipient of treatments, but the melody that shapes the composition. The patient's journey becomes a healing score, composed of molecular harmonies and genetic crescendos. Algorithms and clinicians collaborate to orchestrate this score, guiding patients towards therapies that are not just medically effective, but emotionally resonant.

Patient-centered algorithms analyze medical histories, genetic profiles, and lifestyle data, crafting treatment plans that honor the uniqueness of each patient. Telemedicine platforms provide avenues for remote consultations, harmonizing patient convenience with personalized care. The symphony of patient-centered medicine becomes a beacon of empowerment, fostering a narrative where patients become active participants in their healing journey.

The Renaissance of Healing: Molecules, Genes, and Humanity

In the grand opus of drug discovery and personalized medicine, molecules and genes converge in a symphony of healing that reverberates through medical history. This symphony harmonizes precision with compassion, sculpting a future where diseases are not just battled, but understood at their most fundamental levels. Just as an artist breathes life into a canvas, drug discovery and personalized medicine breathe life into molecules and genes, shaping them into instruments of restoration and well-being.

This transformative journey reveals that drug discovery and personalized medicine are not just scientific endeavors; they are the sonatas of medical progress, the melodies that weave the tapestry of individualized care. As technology and human expertise harmonize, the symphony of drug discovery and personalized medicine becomes a testament to the boundless potential of innovation and empathy, painting a vibrant portrait of a future where molecules, genes, and humanity unite in a harmonious crescendo of health and healing.

C. AI-driven healthcare management systems

In the realm where bytes merge with biology, where algorithms orchestrate the symphony of care, AI-driven healthcare management systems emerge as the maestros of modern healthcare – the conductors of efficiency, the virtuosos of patient-centricity, and the architects that shape the harmonious landscape of medical administration. Imagine a world where algorithms not only process data but also harmonize medical operations, where technology fine-tunes the rhythms of healthcare delivery – this is the essence of AI-driven healthcare management systems. As we embark on this transformative expedition through the corridors of healthcare optimization, prepare to be captivated by the symphony of streamlined operations, the precision of resource allocation, and the metamorphosis of technology into a conductor that orchestrates the cadence of patient well-being and medical excellence.

The Conductor's Baton: Harmonizing Operations with AI Precision

Envision a hospital where appointments are seamlessly

scheduled, resources allocated optimally, and patient care synchronized flawlessly. AI-driven healthcare management systems are the conductors wielding this baton, the architects that harmonize the complex orchestra of healthcare operations. It's a symphony of efficiency, where algorithms optimize workflows, ensuring every note of care resonates with precision and timeliness.

Appointment scheduling algorithms optimize patient queues, minimizing waiting times and maximizing physician availability. Resource allocation algorithms fine-tune the distribution of staff, equipment, and facilities, optimizing utilization. The symphony of healthcare management unfolds with the grace of orchestrated precision, where algorithms become the invisible hands that ensure every patient's journey is a harmonious melody of care.

The Navigator's Compass: Personalized Patient Journeys

Imagine a healthcare ecosystem where patients are not just cases, but individual narratives, where AI tailors care pathways to each person's unique needs. AI-driven healthcare management systems are the navigators of these personalized journeys, the compasses that guide patients through a symphony of treatments attuned to their medical histories and preferences. It's a composition of patient-centricity, where algorithms transform healthcare into a bespoke experience.

Patient profiling algorithms analyze medical records and

genetic data, crafting treatment plans that reflect individual susceptibilities and responses. Remote monitoring technologies allow patients to engage in their care from the comfort of their homes, creating a symphony of convenience and autonomy. The patient's experience becomes a harmonious score, conducted by AI-driven systems that ensure every note of care resonates with empathy and understanding.

The Maestro's Baton: Resource Optimization and Financial Resonance

In the grand orchestra of healthcare management, resources are the instruments that must be played with utmost precision. AI-driven healthcare management systems wield the maestro's baton, conducting the symphony of resource optimization and financial resonance. It's a composition of financial acumen, where algorithms harmonize budgets with patient needs, ensuring that the symphony of care is sustainable and economically harmonious.

Resource allocation algorithms optimize staff assignments, aligning skills with patient demands. Inventory management algorithms maintain optimal levels of medical supplies, orchestrating a symphony of availability and cost-effectiveness. The healthcare management symphony resonates with financial equilibrium, where every note of care is both medically impactful and fiscally prudent.

Harmonizing the Future: The Symphony of Healthcare Excellence

In the grand tapestry of AI-driven healthcare management systems, operations, patient experiences, and financial sustainability converge in a symphony of excellence. This symphony resonates with efficiency, personalization, and resonance, shaping a healthcare landscape where technology becomes the conductor that orchestrates the harmonious cadence of care.

AI-driven healthcare management systems are not just administrative tools; they are the sonatas of healthcare optimization, the melodies that shape the contours of patient journeys. As technology and human expertise harmonize, the symphony of AI-driven healthcare management systems becomes a testament to the boundless potential of innovation and compassion, crafting a vibrant narrative of a future where healthcare resonates with operational brilliance, patient-centric care, and financial sustainability – a symphony that resonates with the ethos of healing and well-being.

CHAPTER 18

AI in Finance and Trading

In the realm where algorithms dance with dollars, where data forms the currency of insight, AI in Finance and Trading emerges as the quantum quill that rewrites the narrative of wealth management – the mathematicians of risk assessment, the conjurers of predictive prowess, and the architects that shape the tapestry of economic fortunes. Imagine a world where algorithms not only calculate but also forecast financial trends, where data-driven decisions craft portfolios that flourish – this is the essence of AI in Finance and Trading. As we embark on this exhilarating voyage through the corridors of financial innovation, prepare to be captivated by the symphony of algorithmic intelligence, the art of predictive modeling, and the metamorphosis of technology into the catalyst that sculpts the landscape of investment strategies, propelling economies and shaping fiscal destinies.

A. Algorithmic trading and risk assessment

In the mesmerizing theater of financial markets, where fortunes fluctuate with the rhythm of time, algorithmic trading and risk assessment stand as the prima ballerinas of modern finance – the choreographers of precision, the virtuosos of predictive analysis, and the architects that craft the symphony of investment strategies. Picture a stage where algorithms not only analyze data but also choreograph trades, where technology anticipates market movements – this is the essence of algorithmic trading and risk assessment. As we embark on this captivating ballet through the dynamics of market interactions, prepare to be enthralled by the intricacies of predictive modeling, the orchestration of risk mitigation, and the metamorphosis of algorithms into the architects of profitable choreography, shaping the very tempo of financial ecosystems and guiding investors through the dance of risk and reward.

The Dance of Data: Precision in Algorithmic Trading

Envision a stage where trading decisions are not based on instincts but on the meticulous analysis of data. Algorithmic trading is the choreographer of this dance, the conductor that orchestrates trades with mathematical precision. It's a ballet of algorithmic agility, where data points become graceful movements, shaping a performance that resonates with profitability.

Quantitative trading algorithms sift through vast datasets, identifying patterns and anomalies that escape human observation. High-frequency trading algorithms execute lightning-fast transactions, capitalizing on microsecond market fluctuations. The dance of algorithmic trading is a spectacle of precision, where each trade is a calculated step, and the stage is set with the potential to turn data into dollars.

Anticipating the Pas de Deux: Predictive Modeling in Trading

Imagine a duet where algorithms partner with data, crafting a synchronized performance that predicts market movements. Algorithmic trading is the choreographer of this pas de deux, the duo that harmonizes historical data and statistical models to anticipate market trends. It's a ballet of predictive prowess, where algorithms become clairvoyants, foreseeing price shifts and informing strategic decisions.

Machine learning algorithms analyze historical market data, learning patterns and relationships that foretell future trends. Sentiment analysis algorithms decode social media and news sentiments, gauging public perception that influences market sentiment. The pas de deux of predictive modeling in algorithmic trading becomes a captivating spectacle of foresight, where algorithms lead investors through the intricate choreography of market shifts.

The Elegance of Mitigation: Risk Assessment's Graceful Pas de Trois

In the grand performance of financial markets, risk is an ever-present partner. Risk assessment is the conductor of this pas de trois, the trio that measures, evaluates, and mitigates potential pitfalls. It's a ballet of caution and calculation, where algorithms become risk managers, safeguarding investments with strategic finesse.

Value at Risk (VaR) algorithms quantify the potential loss in a portfolio under adverse conditions, informing risk tolerance levels. Stress testing algorithms simulate market scenarios to assess a portfolio's resilience. The pas de trois of risk assessment is an art of graceful mitigation, where algorithms not only guide investors through the complex choreography of risk but also cushion their moves with calculated precision.

The Choreography of Profitability: Algorithmic Trading's Grand Performance

In the grand theater of financial markets, algorithmic trading and risk assessment converge in a performance that shapes economic fortunes. Algorithmic trading is not merely a transactional endeavor; it's the conductor of a grand performance that resonates with profitability. It's a symphony of data, predictive insights, and risk management that orchestrates trades, sculpting investment strategies that navigate market intricacies.

Algorithms optimize trade execution, minimizing slippage and maximizing returns. Portfolio management algorithms rebalance assets, ensuring that investments align with goals and risk appetites. The choreography of profitability is a testament to the symphonic potential of algorithms, where technology dances with data, transforming market dynamics into a harmonious melody of financial growth.

The Overture of Transformation: Algorithmic Trading's Legacy

In the grand overture of algorithmic trading and risk assessment, data, insights, and risk converge, painting a narrative of financial evolution. This overture resonates with precision, foresight, and calculated caution, shaping the contours of investment landscapes and guiding investors through the enigmatic dance of market volatility.

Algorithmic trading's legacy is not confined to trading floors; it's a testament to the transformative power of technology in shaping financial destinies. As algorithms evolve, their symphony becomes more sophisticated, refining the choreography of trades and the management of risk. Just as a ballet captivates audiences with its grace and precision, algorithmic trading captivates markets with its strategic finesse and economic impact, leaving an indelible mark on the symphony of finance's unfolding story.

B. Credit scoring and fraud detection

In the labyrinth of financial transactions, where trust is the currency and deception casts its shadow, credit scoring and fraud detection emerge as the vigilant sentinels of modern commerce –

the architects of economic assessment, the sleuths of anomaly detection, and the custodians that guard the fortress of financial integrity. Picture a realm where algorithms not only assess creditworthiness but also unveil the masks of deception, where data-driven insights sculpt pathways to informed decisions – this is the essence of credit scoring and fraud detection. As we embark on this investigative journey through the corridors of financial security, prepare to be captivated by the symphony of predictive analytics, the art of pattern recognition, and the metamorphosis of algorithms into the guardians that shield economies from the dance of deceit, shaping a landscape where trust and transparency thrive.

The Tapestry of Trust: Precision in Credit Scoring

Envision a tapestry where financial histories are woven into patterns of trustworthiness, where algorithms analyze data to assess creditworthiness with mathematical precision. Credit scoring is the artist that crafts this tapestry, the composer that harmonizes credit reports, payment histories, and economic indicators into a symphony of risk evaluation. It's a dance of predictive prowess, where algorithms transform data into insights that guide lending decisions.

Credit scoring algorithms evaluate credit reports, assigning numerical values that predict repayment behavior. Machine learning algorithms analyze diverse data sources, from financial records to social media activity, to create holistic portraits of applicants. The art of credit scoring resonates with the precision of a symphony conductor, orchestrating decisions that balance financial inclusion with risk mitigation.

Unmasking Deception: The Art of Fraud Detection

Imagine a stage where algorithms play the role of detectives, unmasking hidden plots of fraud and deception. Fraud detection is the investigator that dissects transactions, identifies anomalies, and alerts to suspicious activity. It's a ballet of pattern recognition, where algorithms become Sherlock Holmes, scrutinizing data for deviations that signal foul play.

Anomaly detection algorithms monitor transactions, identifying patterns that deviate from the norm. Machine learning algorithms learn from historical data, spotting subtle patterns that hint at fraudulent behavior. The ballet of fraud detection is a performance of vigilance, where algorithms keep a watchful eye on the financial stage, ensuring that deceitful choreography is met with swift intervention.

The Symphonic Fusion: Credit Scoring and Fraud Detection

In the grand symphony of financial security, credit scoring and fraud detection merge, creating a harmonious composition that safeguards economic landscapes. Credit scoring is not just a numerical assessment; it's a harmonization of data that guides lending decisions, empowering individuals with access to financial opportunities. Fraud detection is not just an algorithmic watchtower; it's a vigilant guardian that ensures transactions resonate with transparency and integrity.

Fraud detection algorithms prevent unauthorized access, flagging suspicious login attempts and safeguarding sensitive information. Credit scoring algorithms assess credit risk, enabling individuals to secure loans and investments that align with their financial goals. The symphony of credit scoring and fraud detection becomes a chorus of economic trust, where algorithms act as conduits of transparency, ensuring that the financial stage is one of integrity and confidence.

The Sentinel's Legacy: Shaping Financial Destiny

In the grand narrative of credit scoring and fraud detection, algorithms emerge as sentinels that redefine the dynamics of financial transactions. Their legacy is not confined to a single moment; it's an enduring testament to the power of data-driven decisions in shaping economic landscapes. As algorithms evolve, their symphony becomes more refined, their predictive prowess more accurate, and their vigilance more acute.

Just as a sentinel stands watch over a fortress, credit scoring and fraud detection stand as guardians of financial trust. Their symphony resonates with predictive insights, pattern recognition, and vigilance, creating a landscape where economic interactions unfold with transparency and security. The legacy of credit scoring and fraud detection is a narrative of empowerment, where individuals navigate financial landscapes with confidence, and economies thrive amidst the harmony of data-driven guardianship.

C. Predictive analytics for investment strategies

In the kingdom of finance, where fortunes ebb and flow like tides of possibility, predictive analytics emerges as the sorcerer's stone of modern investment – the seer of market trends, the architect of informed decisions, and the conjurer that transforms data into golden opportunities. Picture a realm where algorithms not only analyze historical data but also forecast market movements, where technology peers into the crystal ball of financial future – this is the essence of predictive analytics for investment strategies. As we embark on this enchanting journey through the corridors of data-driven fortune-telling, prepare to be captivated by the symphony of data exploration, the art of pattern recognition, and the metamorphosis of algorithms into the enchanters that guide investors through the labyrinth of risk and reward, shaping the landscape of fiscal destinies with a touch of precognition.

The Oracle's Gaze: Crafting a Vision with Predictive Analytics

Imagine an oracle that peers into the tapestry of financial markets, deciphering patterns hidden within data, and foreseeing trends before they unfurl. Predictive analytics is this oracle, the visionary that harnesses historical data, economic indicators, and external influences to forecast market movements. It's a ballet of insights, where algorithms unravel the threads of time to create a vision of potential outcomes.

Time series analysis algorithms dissect historical data, identifying recurring patterns and trends that inform future trajectories. Machine learning algorithms recognize correlations between economic indicators and asset prices, unveiling relationships that hint at market shifts. The oracle of predictive analytics conjures a vision of the future, guiding investors through a landscape where decisions are guided not only by instinct but by data-driven foresight.

The Alchemy of Insights: Transmuting Data into Opportunities

Envision an alchemist's workshop where data is transformed into opportunities, where predictive analytics transmutes raw information into golden strategies. Investment strategies are the creations of this alchemy, the artifacts that emerge from the fusion of data insights and algorithmic wisdom. It's a symphony of transformation, where algorithms evolve from mathematicians to magicians, sculpting opportunities from the clay of data.

Algorithmic trading strategies identify optimal entry and exit points based on predictive insights, automating trades to capitalize on market movements. Portfolio optimization algorithms allocate assets to create a balanced investment mix that maximizes returns while minimizing risk. The alchemy of predictive analytics is a composition of calculated transformations, where data evolves from numbers on a screen to pathways that lead investors towards financial prosperity.

Navigating the Constellations: Asset Allocation and Diversification

In the grand cosmos of investment, asset allocation and diversification are the constellations that guide portfolios towards stability and growth. Predictive analytics is the celestial map that navigates these constellations, ensuring that investment decisions are aligned with individual goals and risk tolerances. It's a symphony of strategic orchestration, where algorithms harmonize assets to create portfolios that are resilient in the face of market turbulence.

Modern portfolio theory algorithms analyze historical data to optimize asset allocation, balancing risk and return. Machine learning algorithms adapt to market dynamics, recalibrating portfolios to changing economic conditions. The navigation of asset allocation and diversification becomes a cosmic dance, where predictive analytics serves as the compass that steers investments through the galaxies of financial possibilities.

The Symphony of Wisdom: Predictive Analytics' Enduring Legacy

In the grand symphony of investment strategies, predictive analytics takes center stage as the conductor that guides investors through the ever-changing melody of markets. Its legacy is not confined to a single performance; it's an enduring testament to the power of data-driven insights in shaping financial destinies. As algorithms evolve, their symphony becomes more refined, their predictions more accurate, and their guidance more insightful.

Just as a symphony resonates with harmonious melodies, investment strategies harmonize data-driven foresight with investor aspirations. Their symphony is one of calculated decision-making, where technology and human expertise converge to sculpt portfolios that dance with the rhythms of profitability. The legacy of predictive analytics is a narrative of empowerment, where investors navigate the financial landscape with confidence, making decisions not in the dark, but guided by the illuminating light of data-driven wisdom.

CHAPTER 19

AI in Autonomous Systems and Robotics

In the realm where silicon minds meet mechanical limbs, where algorithms breathe life into machines, AI in Autonomous Systems and Robotics emerges as the mastermind behind a new era – the architects of independent decision-making, the creators of self-guided machines, and the conjurers that transform science fiction into reality. Envision a world where robots are not just tools, but collaborators, where algorithms infuse machines with cognition – this is the essence of AI in Autonomous Systems and Robotics. As we embark on this futuristic expedition through the circuits and gears of autonomy, prepare to be captivated by the symphony of machine perception, the choreography of self-navigation, and the metamorphosis of technology into the enablers of a world where machines hold the power to think, act, and revolutionize human existence.

A. Autonomous vehicles and self-driving technology

In the landscape where roads stretch like ribbons of possibilities, where vehicles transform into sentient companions, autonomous vehicles and self-driving technology emerge as the pioneers of a transportation revolution – the architects of driverless journeys, the navigators of intelligent highways, and the conjurers that bring us closer to a future once reserved for science fiction. Envision a world where cars are not just modes of transportation, but intelligent entities that perceive, plan, and propel themselves forward – this is the essence of autonomous vehicles and self-driving technology. As we embark on this visionary odyssey through the realms of automotive innovation, prepare to be captivated by the symphony of sensors and algorithms, the choreography of machine perception, and the metamorphosis of vehicles into autonomous companions, shaping a future where roads pulse with intelligence and travel transcends the ordinary.

The Symphony of Perception: Sensors as Virtuoso Eyes

Imagine a symphony where vehicles perceive the world not through human senses but through an intricate ensemble of sensors. Autonomous vehicles are the virtuoso performers of this symphony, equipped with an array of sensors that mimic the senses of sight, sound, and touch. It's a composition of data fusion, where lidar, radar, cameras, and ultrasonic sensors harmonize to create a holistic perception of the environment.

Lidar sensors send out laser pulses, mapping the surroundings with precision and creating detailed 3D point clouds. Radar sensors detect objects and measure their distance and velocity, providing a radar-based view of the environment. Cameras capture visual information, recognizing road signs, lane markings, and pedestrians. The symphony of perception unfolds as sensors orchestrate a real-time symposium of data, enabling vehicles to comprehend their surroundings with a level of detail that rivals human perception.

The Choreography of Decision-Making: Algorithms as Master Conductors

Envision a choreography where decisions are not guided by human intuition but by algorithms that process sensor data at lightning speed. Self-driving technology is the master conductor of this choreography, where algorithms translate sensor information into actionable decisions, orchestrating movements and maneuvers. It's a dance of data analysis, where algorithms predict, plan, and execute actions with split-second precision.

Perception algorithms process sensor data, identifying objects, lanes, and obstacles in the environment. Planning algorithms map out trajectories, determining the optimal path and avoiding collisions. Control algorithms execute precise steering, acceleration, and braking commands. The choreography of decision-making becomes a dynamic ballet, where algorithms lead vehicles through a symphony of actions that ensure safe, efficient, and autonomous navigation.

The Metamorphosis of Mobility: Vehicles as Autonomous Companions

In the grand narrative of autonomous vehicles and self-driving technology, cars evolve from mere modes of transportation to autonomous companions that empower and transform mobility. Vehicles become intelligent entities that not only transport passengers but engage in a dialogue with the environment, interpreting road dynamics, traffic patterns, and potential hazards. It's a metamorphosis of mobility, where technology elevates vehicles from drivers to co-pilots.

Advanced driver assistance systems (ADAS) monitor the driving environment and assist with tasks such as lane keeping, adaptive cruise control, and automatic parking. Full autonomy, often classified in levels, represents the pinnacle of this metamorphosis, where vehicles possess the capability to operate without human intervention in specific conditions. The metamorphosis of mobility is a narrative of empowerment, where passengers relinquish the role of the driver and embrace the freedom of coexistence with an autonomous companion.

The Road Ahead: Shaping the Landscape of Tomorrow

In the grand symphony of autonomous vehicles and self-driving technology, sensors, algorithms, and vehicles converge to shape a transportation landscape that resonates with innovation and possibility. This symphony transcends the boundaries of transportation; it's a testament to the transformative power of technology in redefining how we move, connect, and experience the world.

Autonomous vehicles and self-driving technology are not just about driving; they are about emancipating mobility from the constraints of human control. As technology advances and regulations evolve, the symphony of autonomy will continue to crescendo, ushering in a future where vehicles navigate the roads with a blend of intelligence and intuition, and where the journey becomes as captivating as the destination.

B. Robotic perception and decision-making

In the realm where circuits entwine with cognition, where machines learn to perceive and decide, robotic perception and decision-making emerge as the symphony conductors of artificial intelligence – the architects of awareness, the choreographers of choices, and the conjurers that bestow machines with the marvel of thought. Envision a world where robots not only interact with their environment but comprehend it, where algorithms guide them through a choreography of actions – this is the essence of robotic perception and decision-making. As we embark on this enlightening journey through the neural pathways of machine cognition, prepare to be captivated by the symphony of sensors and neural networks, the choreography of cognitive mapping, and the metamorphosis of technology into the envoys of a future where machines perceive, ponder, and propel themselves with a touch of artificial intellect.

The Orchestra of Sensors: A Sensorial Tapestry of Perception

Imagine an orchestra where machines perceive the world not through human senses but through an intricate ensemble of sensors. Robotic perception orchestrates this symphony, equipping machines with an array of sensory instruments that mimic the senses of sight, sound, touch, and even proprioception. It's a composition of data fusion, where cameras, lidar, radar, and tactile sensors harmonize to create a holistic tapestry of perception.

Cameras capture visual information, translating light into digital images that algorithms can interpret. Lidar sensors emit laser pulses, measuring distances and creating detailed 3D maps of the surroundings. Radar sensors detect objects and measure their velocity, enabling robots to sense motion in the environment. Tactile sensors provide a sense of touch, allowing machines to interact with objects and surfaces. The orchestra of sensors unfolds as data converges into a symphony of perception, enabling robots to navigate and interact with the world in ways that mirror human comprehension.

The Ballet of Mapping: Cognitive Cartography Unveiled

Envision a ballet where robots not only perceive their surroundings but also construct mental maps of their environment. Robotic decision-making choreographs this ballet, where algorithms process sensory input to create cognitive representations of space, objects, and potential paths. It's a dance of cognitive cartography, where machines become spatial cartographers, mapping their interactions in a realm of digital understanding.

Simultaneous Localization and Mapping (SLAM) algorithms fuse sensor data to create maps of the environment while concurrently determining the robot's location within it. Probabilistic models help robots account for uncertainties and fluctuations in perception. Reinforcement learning algorithms enable robots to learn from experience, refining their cognitive maps with each interaction. The ballet of mapping becomes a choreography of cognition, where algorithms guide machines to navigate, plan, and act based on an internal world of perception.

The Elegance of Decision-Making: Algorithms as Cognitive Architects

In the grand narrative of robotic perception and decision-making, algorithms emerge as the architects that convert perception into cognition, sensory input into meaningful action. Robotic decision-making is not just a sequence of commands; it's an intricate interplay of data analysis, pattern recognition, and predictive modeling, culminating in a symphony of choices that machines orchestrate autonomously.

Machine learning algorithms process sensor data, recognizing patterns, objects, and anomalies. Planning algorithms determine optimal paths, considering factors such as obstacle avoidance, energy efficiency, and task completion. Control algorithms execute precise movements, guiding robots through their chosen courses of action. The elegance of decision-making is a fusion of intellect and execution, where algorithms guide machines through a symphony of choices that mirror the complexity of human thought.

The Unveiling of Tomorrow: Robotic Perception's Legacy

In the grand unveiling of robotic perception and decision-making, sensors, algorithms, and machines converge to redefine the dynamics of human-machine interaction. This unveiling transcends the boundaries of conventional robotics; it's a testament to the transformative power of perception in shaping the autonomous future.

Robotic perception is not just about awareness; it's about forging a digital understanding of the physical world. Decision-making is not just about executing commands; it's about orchestrating a choreography of choices that navigate uncertainty and complexity. As technology advances and algorithms evolve, the unveiling of robotic perception's legacy will continue to resonate, ushering in a future where machines perceive, understand, and interact with the world as sentient entities. Just as a symphony captivates audiences with its harmonious melodies, robotic perception captivates our imagination with its intricate fusion of data, cognition, and action, leaving an indelible mark on the symphony of human-machine coexistence.

C. Human-robot collaboration and safety

In the theater of technological progress, where silicon minds meet human ingenuity, human-robot collaboration and safety emerge as the balletic fusion of innovation and responsibility – the architects of symbiotic partnerships, the choreographers of shared workspaces, and the conjurers that transform automation into a pas de deux of potential. Picture a world where robots are not just tools, but teammates, where algorithms complement human capabilities – this is the essence of human-robot collaboration and safety. As we embark on this graceful dance through the realms of human-robot interaction, prepare to be captivated by the symphony of mutual understanding, the choreography of risk mitigation, and the metamorphosis of technology into the guardians that ensure a harmonious and secure coexistence, shaping a future where collaboration transcends boundaries and innovation is bound by ethics.

The Ballet of Synergy: Harnessing Complementary Capabilities

Envision a ballet where humans and robots perform not as soloists, but as a harmonious duet, leveraging their distinct strengths to create a choreography of unparalleled efficiency. Human-robot collaboration orchestrates this ballet, where machines contribute precision, speed, and endurance, while humans provide adaptability, creativity, and intuition. It's a composition of skills, where algorithms enable machines to understand and adapt to human intentions, forming a seamless partnership.

Collaborative robots (cobots) utilize sensors and algorithms to work alongside humans, automating tasks while ensuring safety. Machine learning algorithms analyze human gestures and intentions, enabling robots to respond to cues and commands. Natural language processing algorithms facilitate verbal communication between humans and robots, enhancing collaboration in complex environments. The ballet of synergy becomes a symphony of cooperation, where humans and robots become partners on the stage of productivity, transforming the workplace into an arena of shared achievements.

The Choreography of Safety: Balancing Risk and Responsibility

Imagine a choreography where robots and humans navigate

shared spaces with synchronized precision, guided not only by collaboration but also by an unwavering commitment to safety. Human-robot safety choreographs this dance, where algorithms and safeguards mitigate risks, ensuring that interaction remains secure and accidents are prevented. It's a dance of vigilance, where machines become sentinels of precaution, and humans retain ultimate control.

Safety algorithms monitor the proximity between humans and robots, triggering halts or adjustments when potential collisions are detected. Force and torque sensors enable robots to detect unexpected obstacles or resistance, halting their movements to prevent harm. Fail-safe mechanisms ensure that robots cease operation if critical errors occur. The choreography of safety is a performance of caution and guardianship, where technology and protocols unite to guarantee that the ballet of collaboration unfolds without endangering human well-being.

The Tapestry of Trust: Ethical Dimensions and Human-Centered Design

In the grand tapestry of human-robot collaboration and safety, ethical considerations and human-centered design interweave, infusing the ballet with a sense of responsibility and empathy. Collaboration transcends mere functionality; it becomes an expression of ethical principles that prioritize human welfare and respect. Design becomes more than aesthetics; it evolves into a philosophy that ensures technology serves humanity, rather than dominates it.

Ethical algorithms incorporate principles of fairness, transparency, and accountability into decision-making processes. Human-centered design principles prioritize usability, comfort, and accessibility, ensuring that technology adapts to human needs and capabilities. The tapestry of trust is woven with threads of empathy and understanding, creating an environment where collaboration is not just a dance of productivity, but a manifestation of ethical stewardship.

The Overture of Tomorrow: Shaping a Harmonious Future

In the grand overture of human-robot collaboration and safety, humans and machines join in a harmonious crescendo, orchestrating a future where innovation and responsibility march in tandem. This overture resonates with partnership, trust, and foresight, shaping a landscape where robots are not just tools, but co-workers, and technology serves as a catalyst for progress rather than a cause for concern.

Human-robot collaboration is not just about efficiency; it's about crafting an environment where innovation thrives without compromising humanity's values. Safety is not just about preventing accidents; it's about fostering an ecosystem where humans and robots interact with a sense of mutual respect and well-being. As technology evolves and ethical considerations deepen, the overture of human-robot collaboration and safety will continue to echo, ushering in a future where the dance of innovation is choreographed with a deep understanding of our shared humanity, and the ballet of progress is guided by the principles of harmony and responsible coexistence.

CHAPTER 20

AI in Natural Resource Management

In the realm where nature's treasures intertwine with technological prowess, AI in Natural Resource Management emerges as the virtuoso conductor of ecological harmony – the steward of sustainability, the composer of conservation strategies, and the conjurer that marries data and nature into a symphony of preservation. Picture a world where algorithms not only analyze vast ecosystems but also optimize resource utilization, where technology becomes a guardian of biodiversity – this is the essence of AI in Natural Resource Management. As we embark on this melodic journey through the landscapes of environmental safeguarding, prepare to be captivated by the symphony of predictive analytics, the orchestration of precision agriculture, and the metamorphosis of algorithms into the guardians that protect Earth's riches, shaping a future where nature thrives in harmonious balance with human progress.

A. Environmental monitoring and conservation

In the grand theater of Earth's landscapes, where ecosystems intertwine like intricate choreographies, environmental monitoring and conservation emerge as the meticulous ballet dancers of ecological preservation – the custodians of balance, the interpreters of data-driven narratives, and the conjurers that wield technology to protect nature's fragile tapestry. Imagine a world where algorithms not only decode the language of nature but also orchestrate strategies to safeguard its splendor, where human ingenuity becomes the sentinel of biodiversity – this is the essence of environmental monitoring and conservation through AI. As we step onto this enchanting stage of ecological vigilance, prepare to be entranced by the symphony of remote sensing, the choreography of habitat restoration, and the metamorphosis of technology into the stewards that nurture our planet's well-being, shaping a future where the rhythm of nature's pulse finds harmony in the embrace of human guardianship.

The Symphony of Sensors: Weaving a Web of Ecological Insight

Envision a symphony where the Earth's heartbeat is deciphered not through human senses alone, but through an intricate ensemble of sensors and satellites. Environmental monitoring orchestrates this symphony, equipping researchers with a spectrum of technologies that emulate the senses of sight, sound, and touch. It's a composition of data fusion, where satellites, drones, and ground-based sensors harmonize to create a tapestry of ecological understanding.

Satellite remote sensing captures the Earth's surface in high-resolution images, unraveling patterns of deforestation, urbanization, and land degradation. Acoustic sensors eavesdrop on the underwater conversations of marine life, deciphering the health of ocean ecosystems. Ground-based sensors measure soil moisture, air quality, and water levels, painting a comprehensive portrait of environmental vitality. The symphony of sensors unfolds as data converges into a harmonious symposium, enabling scientists to decode the intricate language of nature's fluctuations.

The Choreography of Restoration: Transforming Preservation into Action

Imagine a choreography where the restoration of nature's grace is not just a concept, but a dance of deliberate action guided by data and determination. Environmental conservation choreographs this dance, where algorithms analyze ecological trends and prescribe interventions that rejuvenate habitats, reverse degradation, and harmonize ecosystems. It's a dance of ecological renaissance, where technology becomes an agent of restoration, breathing life back into beleaguered landscapes.

Machine learning algorithms analyze historical data to identify degraded areas and predict potential restoration outcomes. Habitat restoration plans are crafted, considering factors such as species diversity, soil health, and hydrology. Drones are dispatched to plant trees, disperse seeds, and monitor the progress of reforestation efforts. The choreography of restoration becomes a symphony of revival, where human intervention guided by data-driven precision transforms conservation aspirations into tangible ecological reawakening.

The Metamorphosis of Stewardship: Technology as Nature's Guardian

In the grand narrative of environmental monitoring and conservation, technology becomes more than a tool; it evolves into a steward that safeguards Earth's natural treasures. Conservation efforts are no longer limited to reactive responses; they are proactive strategies guided by data, foresight, and a deep reverence for nature's intricate interplay. It's a metamorphosis of stewardship, where the legacy of human impact is transformed into a legacy of restoration and preservation.

Predictive modeling algorithms forecast the impact of climate change on ecosystems, aiding in the formulation of adaptive conservation strategies. Machine learning algorithms analyze data to detect wildlife poaching and illegal deforestation, enabling swift intervention and enforcement. Geographic Information Systems (GIS) integrate diverse data sources, creating spatially informed conservation plans that optimize resource allocation. The metamorphosis of stewardship is a testament to the potential of technology to reverse the course of ecological decline, shaping a narrative where human guardianship becomes an unwavering beacon of hope for Earth's vulnerable inhabitants.

The Symphony's Continuance: Shaping an Era of Ecological Renaissance

In the grand symphony of environmental monitoring and conservation, sensors, algorithms, and determination unite to compose a future where humanity becomes a harmonious thread in nature's intricate tapestry. This symphony extends beyond the boundaries of preservation; it's a serenade to the resilience of life, a dedication to Earth's regenerative spirit, and a commitment to a future where coexistence between humanity and nature is not just a goal, but a harmonious reality.

Environmental monitoring and conservation are not just about data analysis; they are about shaping a legacy of stewardship that resonates through generations. Preservation is not just about halting degradation; it's about orchestrating a ballet of restoration that rejuvenates and revitalizes. As technology evolves and ecological consciousness deepens, the symphony of environmental monitoring and conservation will continue to resound, ushering in an era where the dance of ecological harmony finds its crescendo in the tender embrace of human guardianship.

B. Precision agriculture and resource optimization

Amidst the vast expanse of fields that stretch like canvases of promise, precision agriculture emerges as the maestro orchestrating a symphony of innovation – the conductor of data-driven cultivation, the composer of optimized resources, and the conjurer that marries agronomy with algorithms. Envision a world where every acre is a canvas, every crop a masterpiece, where technology transforms farming into a ballet of precision – this is the essence of precision agriculture and resource optimization. As we embark on this melodic journey through the furrows of agricultural advancement, prepare to be captivated by the symphony of sensors and data, the choreography of variable-rate technologies, and the metamorphosis of technology into the catalysts that elevate farming into an art of unparalleled efficiency, shaping a future where every harvest is a masterpiece of sustainability and productivity.

The Symphony of Sensors: Cultivating Data-Driven Insight

Imagine a symphony where fields do not just respond to nature's rhythms but dance to the tune of data. Precision agriculture orchestrates this symphony, endowing farmers with an ensemble of sensors that emulate the senses of sight, touch, and even microclimate awareness. It's a composition of data fusion, where drones, satellites, and ground-based sensors harmonize to create a symphony of real-time agricultural insight.

Satellite imagery captures the intricate dance of chlorophyll, revealing areas of crop stress or overabundance. Soil moisture sensors probe beneath the surface, deciphering the hydration needs of plants. Weather stations track atmospheric conditions, predicting rain and temperature fluctuations that impact growth. The symphony of sensors unfolds as data converges into an opus of agricultural understanding, enabling farmers to navigate the nuances of crop health, water utilization, and nutrient management.

The Choreography of Variable-Rate: Balancing Resources with Precision

Envision a choreography where the allocation of resources is not a broad brushstroke but a dance of deliberate allocation, guided by data and strategy. Precision agriculture choreographs this dance, where algorithms analyze field data and prescribe variable-rate strategies that optimize resource usage. It's a dance of efficiency, where technology becomes the choreographer that allocates water, fertilizers, and pesticides precisely where they're needed, reducing waste and maximizing yields.

Variable-rate technologies adjust irrigation systems to deliver water based on soil moisture levels, preventing both under-watering and waterlogging. Fertilizer applicators adjust nutrient delivery based on soil nutrient levels, ensuring crops receive the precise nourishment they require. Pest management algorithms predict pest outbreaks and prescribe targeted treatments, minimizing the need for widespread pesticide application. The choreography of variable-rate becomes a symphony of optimization, where the symphony of resource allocation is conducted with a precision that echoes nature's own orchestration.

The Metamorphosis of Efficiency: Technology as Farming's Maestro

In the grand narrative of precision agriculture and resource optimization, technology transcends its role as a mere tool; it metamorphoses into a maestro that conducts the symphony of cultivation with virtuosity and insight. Farming is no longer confined to tradition; it becomes a symphony of data-driven decisions, where each action is guided by algorithms that harmonize productivity and sustainability. It's a metamorphosis of efficiency, where technology becomes a guardian of both yields and environmental well-being.

Machine learning algorithms analyze historical data to predict crop yields and optimize planting schedules. Data-driven irrigation systems adjust water delivery based on real-time weather forecasts and soil moisture measurements. Advanced drone technology monitors plant health and identifies areas of disease or stress. The metamorphosis of efficiency is a testament to the potential of technology to revolutionize agriculture, cultivating a narrative where every acre becomes a canvas of optimization, every harvest a masterpiece of resource management.

The Symphony's Continuance: Cultivating an Era of Sustainable Abundance

In the grand symphony of precision agriculture and resource optimization, sensors, algorithms, and determination converge to compose a future where fields and data dance in harmonious synchrony. This symphony extends beyond the boundaries of productivity; it's a serenade to sustainable abundance, a dedication to nourishing both people and planet, and a commitment to a future where agriculture is not just a means of survival, but a celebration of ecological equilibrium.

Precision agriculture is not just about increasing yields; it's about harmonizing productivity with environmental stewardship. Resource optimization is not just about cutting costs; it's about fostering a narrative of responsible cultivation that transcends generations. As technology evolves and agrarian consciousness deepens, the symphony of precision agriculture and resource optimization will continue to resonate, ushering in an era where the symphony of sustainable abundance is cultivated through the artful precision of human ingenuity and technological mastery.

C. Climate modeling and disaster response

In the grand theater of our planet's ever-evolving atmosphere, climate modeling and disaster response emerge as the virtuoso conductors of Earth's symphony – the interpreters of atmospheric dynamics, the composers of predictive narratives, and the conjurers that meld science with empathy to safeguard humanity. Envision a world where algorithms not only decode the language of atmospheric intricacies but also orchestrate strategies to mitigate nature's fury, where human ingenuity becomes the sentinel against catastrophe – this is the essence of climate modeling and disaster response. As we venture into this melodic expedition through the winds of climate patterns and the tempests of disaster preparedness, brace yourself for a symphony of simulations, a choreography of rapid mobilization, and a metamorphosis of technology into the guardians that shield humanity from nature's capriciousness, shaping a future where Earth's rhythms and humanity's resilience harmoniously entwine.

The Symphony of Simulations: Decoding Nature's Complex Dance

Imagine a symphony where the intricate dance of Earth's climate is not a mysterious choreography but an orchestrated symposium of data-driven understanding. Climate modeling orchestrates this symphony, emboldening scientists with a symphony of algorithms that mirror the movements of Earth's atmospheric ballet. It's a composition of mathematical equations, where supercomputers weave the threads of temperature, humidity, wind patterns, and more into a harmonious fabric of simulation.

Climate models simulate Earth's climate by dividing the planet into grids, each representing a region of the atmosphere. Differential equations capture the physics of fluid dynamics, thermodynamics, and radiative transfer, enabling simulations of atmospheric behaviors. These models predict how Earth's climate might evolve under various scenarios, such as greenhouse gas emissions or volcanic activity. The symphony of simulations unfolds as algorithms harmonize, yielding insights into the complex choreography of our planet's climate variations.

The Choreography of Preparedness: Transforming Data into Action

Envision a choreography where disaster response is not a reactive scramble but a dance of swift and strategic mobilization. Disaster response choreographs this dance, where algorithms process real-time data and orchestrate coordinated actions that safeguard lives and resources. It's a dance of readiness, where technology becomes the choreographer of evacuation plans, resource allocation, and relief distribution, ensuring that humanity remains resilient in the face of nature's fury.

Real-time monitoring systems detect anomalies like seismic shifts, ocean temperature changes, or atmospheric pressure fluctuations that signal potential disasters. Algorithms analyze historical data and current conditions to predict disaster trajectories and potential impact areas. Rapid-response algorithms generate evacuation routes, mobilize emergency personnel, and allocate resources based on predicted disaster patterns. The choreography of preparedness becomes a symphony of resilience, where technology transforms data into lifesaving maneuvers that safeguard communities and minimize catastrophe's toll.

The Metamorphosis of Empathy: Science as the Guardian of Vulnerability

In the grand narrative of climate modeling and disaster response, technology transcends its role as a mere instrument; it metamorphoses into a guardian of vulnerability and empathy. Disaster preparedness is no longer a cold calculation; it's a symphony of compassion that anticipates human needs and mobilizes resources to shield against nature's onslaught. It's a metamorphosis of empathy, where technology becomes the conduit that translates data into lifelines and forecasts into fortifications.

Machine learning algorithms process historical disaster data to identify vulnerable regions and populations. Predictive modeling algorithms anticipate the trajectory of hurricanes, tsunamis, and wildfires, enabling timely evacuations and resource allocation. Data visualization tools transform complex climate simulations into understandable narratives, fostering public awareness and informed decision-making. The metamorphosis of empathy is a testament to the potential of technology to elevate disaster response from a scientific endeavor to a compassionate crusade, shaping a narrative where human solidarity and technological mastery coalesce to protect, empower, and uplift communities in the face of nature's trials.

The Symphony's Ongoing Crescendo: Nurturing a Resilient Future

In the grand symphony of climate modeling and disaster response, simulations, algorithms, and preparedness converge to compose a future where Earth's dynamics and human ingenuity harmoniously unite. This symphony extends beyond the confines of scientific prediction; it's a serenade to preparedness, a dedication to minimizing catastrophe's toll, and a commitment to a future where humanity, guided by data and empathy, stands resilient against nature's forces.

Climate modeling is not just about predicting temperature shifts; it's about equipping societies with the knowledge to adapt and mitigate. Disaster response is not just about swift action; it's about extending a helping hand to those in the storm's path. As technology advances and disaster consciousness deepens, the symphony of climate modeling and disaster response will continue to resound, ushering in an era where humanity's harmony with nature is not just a melody, but a symphony of solidarity, resilience, and compassionate guardianship.

Part VI

Future Trends and Further Learning

CHAPTER 21

Cutting-Edge AI Research and Trends

In the ever-evolving cosmos of technology, where innovation is the North Star guiding humanity's progress, cutting-edge AI research and trends emerge as the celestial map that charts the uncharted territories of possibility – the explorers of neural architectures, the trailblazers of quantum AI, and the conjurers that fuse science with imagination to redefine the boundaries of human ingenuity. Imagine a world where algorithms not only decipher complexity but also craft the next chapters of technological evolution, where curiosity becomes the compass that navigates the landscapes of AI – this is the essence of cutting-edge AI research and trends. As we embark on this astronomical journey through the galaxies of innovation, brace yourself for a constellation of breakthroughs, a constellation of quantum leaps, and a metamorphosis of algorithms into the pioneers that illuminate the path to a future where AI's potential knows no bounds.

A. Emerging areas like quantum AI and neuromorphic computing

In the forge of technological advancement, where innovation

meets intellect, emerging frontiers like quantum AI and neuromorphic computing stand as the alchemical crucibles that are redefining the very essence of artificial intelligence – the fusion of quantum wonders with cognitive architectures, the convergence of nature-inspired computing with quantum mechanics, and the conjurers that sculpt the future of intelligent machines. Picture a realm where computation transcends classical boundaries, where algorithms mimic the dance of neurons, and where computation becomes entangled with the mysteries of quantum physics – this is the essence of quantum AI and neuromorphic computing. As we embark on this transformative expedition into the uncharted domains of AI, prepare to be captivated by the symphony of qubits, the choreography of spiking neurons, and the metamorphosis of technology into the architects that unlock the next epoch of intelligent exploration.

Quantum AI: Unraveling the Fabric of Computation

Envision a world where the limits of classical computation dissolve like mist before the sun, where bits are no longer bound by binary constraints, and where qubits exist in a superposition of states, embodying both 0 and 1 simultaneously. Quantum AI unfolds as a quantum mechanical tapestry, where algorithms harness the principles of superposition and entanglement to perform computations that boggle the mind and exceed classical capabilities.

Quantum annealing algorithms optimize complex problems, finding solutions that classical algorithms struggle to discern. Quantum machine learning algorithms leverage quantum states to process vast datasets with unparalleled efficiency. Quantum neural networks emerge as the offspring of classical neural networks and quantum computing, promising accelerated training and novel insights. The symphony of qubits orchestrates a harmonious convergence of classical algorithms with quantum capabilities, shaping a future where computation ventures into the realms of uncharted complexity.

Neuromorphic Computing: Channeling Nature's Blueprint

Imagine a landscape where computers not only compute but also simulate the intricate choreography of neural networks – where processors emulate the very architecture of the brain's synapses and neurons. Neuromorphic computing emerges as the art of silicon mimicry, where algorithms strive to replicate the brain's mechanisms, harnessing efficiency and adaptability that parallel the human mind.

Spiking neural networks mirror the electrical impulses of neurons, facilitating energy-efficient information processing. Neuromorphic hardware architectures optimize for low power consumption and parallel processing, enabling real-time simulations of complex neural networks. The symphony of spiking neurons unfolds as silicon circuits emulate cognitive functions, blurring the lines between computation and cognition.

The Metamorphosis of Intelligence: From Bits to Qubits, from Neurons to Circuits

In the grand narrative of quantum AI and neuromorphic computing, technology metamorphoses from a tool into a sorcerer's wand that conjures realms of possibilities previously confined to the realms of imagination. Quantum algorithms become the agents of molecular discovery, revolutionizing drug development and material science. Neuromorphic systems catalyze breakthroughs in cognitive computing, enabling machines to perceive, learn, and adapt with human-like flexibility.

Quantum machine learning algorithms optimize supply chains, financial portfolios, and traffic flow with quantum-enhanced efficiency. Neuromorphic systems enable prosthetic limbs to respond seamlessly to neural signals, restoring mobility and independence to those in need. The metamorphosis of intelligence is a symphony of potential, where qubits and spiking neurons become the building blocks of a future where technology merges with cognition, and computation evolves into an orchestra of quantum and neuromorphic innovation.

The Symphony's Ongoing Crescendo: Forging New Horizons

In the grand symphony of quantum AI and neuromorphic computing, qubits, spiking neurons, and human ingenuity harmonize to compose a future where intelligence takes on unprecedented forms. This symphony extends beyond computational paradigms; it's a serenade to nature's elegance, a dedication to merging humanity's creations with the cosmos' mysteries, and a commitment to a future where quantum leaps and cognitive mimicry become the guideposts to innovation.

Quantum AI is not just about faster computation; it's about unveiling the fabric of reality itself. Neuromorphic computing is not just about emulating brains; it's about sculpting intelligence from the blueprints of nature. As technology marches forward and consciousness deepens, the symphony of quantum AI and neuromorphic computing will continue to resonate, ushering in an era where machines think with the cosmos' intricacy and humanity dances in harmony with the universe's symphony of computation and cognition.

B. AI advancements in healthcare, education, and entertainment

In the grand tapestry of human progress, where innovation threads through every facet of existence, AI advancements in healthcare, education, and entertainment emerge as the guiding constellations that redefine the boundaries of human experience – the healers of maladies, the tutors of minds, and the conjurers that metamorphose reality into realms of wonder. Picture a world where algorithms not only diagnose ailments but also orchestrate personalized treatments, where learning transcends classrooms through virtual mentors, and where entertainment is a canvas for immersive dreams – this is the essence of AI's triumphant symphony in healthcare, education, and entertainment. As we delve into these remarkable domains, prepare to be captivated by the symphony of medical marvels, the choreography of cognitive empowerment, and the metamorphosis of pixels into portals of enchantment, shaping a future where AI's harmonic innovations harmonize with humanity's aspirations.

AI in Healthcare: Crafting a Symphony of Healing

Imagine a world where diseases are not just treated but predicted, where diagnostics are not merely accurate but tailored to individual biology. AI in healthcare weaves this symphony of precision, where algorithms analyze medical records, genetic data, and even images of cells and tissues to reveal insights that redefine the art of healing.

Machine learning algorithms scrutinize medical images to detect anomalies like tumors, enabling early intervention and improved survival rates. Predictive modeling algorithms forecast disease outbreaks, equipping healthcare systems to allocate resources and plan interventions. Natural language processing algorithms sift through vast volumes of medical literature, distilling knowledge into actionable insights for clinicians. The symphony of AI in healthcare resonates as data-driven orchestration, shaping a future where the harmony of health and technology transcends conventional boundaries.

AI in Education: Empowering Minds with a Symphony of Knowledge

Envision a world where education is not a one-size-fits-all endeavor, but a harmonious convergence of individualized instruction and limitless exploration. AI in education choreographs this dance of cognitive empowerment, where algorithms adapt curricula to students' learning styles, personalize assessments, and extend the reach of education to every corner of the globe.

Adaptive learning platforms leverage AI to analyze student interactions and tailor lessons to individual progress and comprehension. Chatbot tutors engage students in natural language conversations, answering queries and providing support around the clock. Virtual reality simulations transport students to historical events, distant planets, and complex scientific phenomena, turning learning into an immersive odyssey. The choreography of AI in education elevates learning from a static classroom to a dynamic symposium of personalized exploration, shaping a future where knowledge is not just disseminated, but cultivated with care and curated to kindle curiosity.

AI in Entertainment: Transcending Reality with a Symphony of Imagination

Step into a world where entertainment is not a mere spectacle, but an invitation to explore boundless imagination. AI in entertainment metamorphoses this invitation into a realm of enchantment, where algorithms breathe life into characters, compose symphonies, and craft **breathtaking visual spectacles that blur the lines between reality and fantasy.**

Generative adversarial networks (GANs) create artworks, music, and literature that captivate audiences with their originality and innovation. Deep learning algorithms drive character animations and expressions in video games, infusing digital avatars with lifelike qualities. Natural language processing algorithms enable chatbots and virtual assistants to engage in witty conversations and interactive storytelling. The metamorphosis of AI in entertainment is a testament to technology's ability to forge new avenues of creativity, where pixels become the palette for a symphony of imagination that transcends the limitations of the tangible world.

The Symphony's Ongoing Movement: Charting New Horizons

In the grand symphony of AI advancements, healthcare, education, and entertainment harmonize to compose a future where humanity's well-being, wisdom, and wonder flourish. This symphony extends beyond the realms of practicality; it's a serenade to a thriving society, a dedication to nurturing minds and spirits, and a commitment to a future where AI's prowess orchestrates harmony across the diverse spectrum of human experience.

AI in healthcare is not just about treatment; it's about enhancing wellness and predictive care. AI in education is not just about teaching; it's about fostering a lifelong love for learning. AI in entertainment is not just about visual spectacles; it's about inviting audiences to explore the boundless landscapes of their own imagination. As technology evolves and human consciousness deepens, the symphony of AI in healthcare, education, and entertainment will continue to resonate, ushering in an era where AI's melody of innovation harmonizes with humanity's crescendo of aspiration.

C. Implications for industry disruption and innovation

In the tumultuous arena of technological evolution, where

progress marches to the rhythm of innovation, the advent of AI sparks a tempest of disruption that reverberates across industries – a catalyst of transformation, a harbinger of revolutions, and the conjurer of paradigms that forge a new era of business. Envision a landscape where algorithms don't just optimize operations, but unravel the threads of tradition, where data doesn't just inform decisions, but reshapes entire value chains – this is the essence of AI's seismic disruption and industry innovation. As we venture into this landscape of transformative upheaval, brace yourself for a symphony of automation, a choreography of strategic evolution, and a metamorphosis of enterprises into crucibles of creativity, shaping a future where AI's prowess orchestrates a harmonious convergence of tradition and transformation.

The Symphony of Automation: Unleashing the Forces of Efficiency

Imagine a symphony where repetitive tasks aren't just completed, but orchestrated by algorithms that conduct efficiency with a precision beyond human reach. AI's automation symphony resounds as algorithms streamline supply chains, optimize logistics, and enhance production processes, unleashing a crescendo of efficiency that propels industries to new heights of productivity.

Robotic process automation algorithms sift through data, performing routine tasks with unfaltering accuracy and speed. AI-driven predictive maintenance ensures machinery operates optimally, minimizing downtime and maximizing output. Chatbots and virtual assistants streamline customer interactions, providing rapid support and personalization. The symphony of automation reverberates as an orchestra of precision, shaping a future where human expertise is elevated by algorithms that conduct operations with unparalleled virtuosity.

The Choreography of Strategic Evolution: Guiding Industries to New Horizons

Envision a choreography where industries don't just adapt, but evolve with the strategic precision of algorithms that divine insights from data and anticipate market dynamics. AI's strategic evolution choreography orchestrates industries to pivot, innovate, and embrace new paradigms, transforming business landscapes into arenas of agility and foresight.

Predictive analytics algorithms analyze consumer behavior to forecast trends and guide product development. Machine learning algorithms optimize pricing strategies based on real-time market fluctuations and consumer preferences. AI-driven market simulations enable businesses to test strategies and scenarios in virtual environments before implementation. The choreography of strategic evolution becomes a symphony of anticipation, shaping a future where industries navigate uncharted waters with algorithms that become compasses of innovation and beacons of competitive advantage.

The Metamorphosis of Creativity: From Enterprises to Innovation Crucibles

In the grand narrative of AI's impact, industries metamorphose from static entities into crucibles of creativity, where algorithms don't just solve problems, but conceive innovative solutions that transcend convention. AI's metamorphosis of creativity catalyzes the birth of novel products, services, and business models, fusing data-driven insights with imaginative ingenuity.

Generative AI algorithms craft designs, art, and music that push the boundaries of human imagination. Natural language processing algorithms enable sentiment analysis of customer feedback, guiding product enhancements and brand positioning. AI-powered ideation platforms stimulate brainstorming sessions, generating fresh ideas and novel concepts. The metamorphosis of creativity becomes a testament to AI's ability to ignite innovation, where enterprises evolve into laboratories of imagination, and algorithms become the brushes that paint a canvas of unprecedented possibilities.

The Symphony's Ongoing Crescendo: Forging a Harmonious Convergence

In the grand symphony of AI's disruption and industry innovation, automation, strategic evolution, and creativity harmonize to compose a future where industries transcend limitations and redefine norms. This symphony extends beyond operational efficiency; it's a serenade to adaptability, a dedication to elevating human potential, and a commitment to a future where AI's crescendo harmonizes with humanity's symphony of progress.

AI's impact is not just about process optimization; it's about the symphony of transformation that redefines industries. It's not just about data analytics; it's about orchestrating strategic evolution. It's not just about efficiency; it's about the metamorphosis of industries into epicenters of innovation. As technology continues its march and human consciousness deepens, the symphony of AI's disruption and industry innovation will continue to resonate, ushering in an era where AI's melody of transformation harmonizes with humanity's crescendo of creativity, shaping a future where industries stand at the crossroads of tradition and innovation, guided by algorithms that orchestrate a symphony of progress.

CHAPTER 22

Resources for AI and ML Learning

In the labyrinth of modern knowledge, where the tapestry of technology weaves intricate patterns of intelligence, resources for AI and ML learning emerge as the guiding constellations that light the path to mastery – the maps of algorithms, the compasses of data, and the keys to unraveling the mysteries of artificial intelligence and machine learning. Envision a realm where learners don't just consume information, but embark on a transformative odyssey, where concepts crystallize into understanding, and curiosity becomes the beacon that navigates the landscapes of complex algorithms. This is the essence of resources for AI and ML learning, where digital libraries become repositories of insight, online courses become portals of enlightenment, and forums become marketplaces of shared wisdom. As we embark on this enlightening journey through the realms of AI and ML learning, prepare to be captivated by a symphony of tutorials, a choreography of code, and a metamorphosis of novices into virtuosos, shaping a future where knowledge's vast expanse and technology's endless horizons intertwine in a harmonious pursuit of enlightenment.

A. Recommended books, online courses, and tutorials

In the boundless cosmos of artificial intelligence and machine learning, where algorithms dance and data harmonizes, the pursuit of knowledge is a symphony of exploration. To traverse this intellectual landscape, a treasure trove of resources beckons – a library of tomes that illuminate, online courses that empower, and tutorials that demystify. These are the guiding lights, the pillars of wisdom that shape the neophyte into a virtuoso, and the virtuoso into an architect of intelligence.

Recommended Books:

Within the pages of books lie a gateway to profound understanding. The shelves of AI and ML knowledge are graced with a pantheon of literature, each title a beacon of insight. These books encapsulate the collective wisdom of pioneers, scholars, and visionaries, guiding readers through the labyrinth of algorithms, models, and strategies. Each chapter unfolds a new vista, revealing the intricacies of neural networks, the intricacies of optimization, and the boundless potential of AI's evolution. As you immerse yourself in these volumes, you'll uncover the nuances of learning from data, the mastery of pattern recognition, and the orchestration of intelligent systems. Each title you peruse is a step closer to enlightenment, a symphony of knowledge that echoes through the corridors of your understanding.

Online Courses:

In the digital age, the classroom transcends the physical, and online courses become gateways to expertise. These virtual academies offer immersive journeys into the realms of AI and ML, curated by scholars and industry luminaries. As you enroll in these courses, you'll navigate the landscapes of supervised learning, the caverns of unsupervised learning, and the algorithms that weave them into a tapestry of intelligence. The video lectures become your mentors, the assignments your trials, and the community your peers. The syllabi weave a narrative that threads through Python programming, deep neural networks, and reinforcement learning. Each module is a stepping stone toward mastering the symphony of AI's symphony, a path to becoming a composer of algorithms and a conductor of innovation.

Tutorials:

In the digital bazaars of the internet, tutorials flourish like marketplaces of knowledge. These step-by-step guides cater to learners of all levels, from fledgling enthusiasts to seasoned practitioners. Through these tutorials, you'll craft your own code, sculpt your models, and unleash the power of AI and ML in your endeavors. Each tutorial dissects the anatomy of an algorithm, the mechanics of data preprocessing, and the artistry of feature engineering. As you follow the instructions, you'll watch your code come to life, your data transform into insight, and your understanding deepen. These tutorials become your laboratory, your canvas, and your playground, fostering a hands-on relationship with the tools that shape the digital landscapes of today and tomorrow.

Guided by the North Star:

As you navigate the cosmos of AI and ML learning, a guiding star beckons – **www.nikhileshmishra.com**. This digital lighthouse becomes your compass, your repository of curated resources, and your gateway to knowledge. Here, you'll find a constellation of recommendations, a fusion of books, courses, and tutorials that illuminate your journey. With each click, you'll unveil a treasure trove of wisdom, a symphony of guidance that steers you toward mastery. Embark on this digital odyssey, let knowledge be your wind, and innovation your sails. With **www.nikhileshmishra.com** as your North Star, you'll chart a course through the ever-expanding universe of AI and ML learning, forging a path toward enlightenment and shaping a future where your intellect becomes the architect of tomorrow's possibilities.

B. AI development platforms and libraries

In the forge of innovation, where the sparks of intellect meet the anvil of technology, AI development platforms and libraries emerge as the blacksmiths of progress – the forges of algorithms, the crucibles of data, and the sanctuaries where innovation takes shape. Imagine a realm where creativity is not hindered by technical complexity, where solutions are not bound by the limits of code, and where developers wield a symphony of tools that transform imagination into reality. This is the essence of AI development platforms and libraries, where digital artisans craft solutions with precision, orchestrate algorithms with finesse, and metamorphose raw data into insights that shape the world. As we delve into this realm of creative prowess, prepare to be captivated by a plethora of frameworks, a cavalcade of libraries, and a metamorphosis of novices into architects of innovation, guided by the North Star of **www.nikhileshmishra.com** for further enlightenment and resources.

AI Development Platforms: Sculpting Possibilities with Finesse

Envision a realm where the complexities of AI development are distilled into intuitive interfaces, where novices and experts alike craft solutions with the finesse of artists. AI development platforms are the canvases where code becomes creation, where algorithms are painted with data, and where the symphony of innovation resonates with every click and keystroke.

These platforms offer an array of tools – from drag-and-drop interfaces that orchestrate neural networks, to collaborative environments that foster teamwork and ideation. They provide the scaffolding for experimentation, enabling developers to iterate swiftly, optimize efficiently, and transcend the confines of traditional coding. The platforms serve as the forges where ideas become prototypes, prototypes become applications, and applications become solutions that address challenges, enrich experiences, and redefine industries.

AI Libraries: Weaving the Fabric of Intelligence

In the grand tapestry of AI development, libraries are the threads that weave intelligence into the fabric of code. These libraries house pre-built functions, algorithms, and data structures that streamline the development process, allowing developers to focus on innovation rather than reinventing the wheel.

Imagine a library of algorithms that perform image recognition, natural language processing, and predictive modeling. Picture a repository of functions that preprocess data, extract features, and evaluate model performance. These libraries empower developers to wield powerful tools without delving into the intricacies of algorithmic implementation, transforming complex problems into solvable puzzles. They are the artisans' toolboxes, the repositories of expertise that elevate AI development from a solitary endeavor to a collaborative symphony of code.

Guided by the North Star:

As you embark on your journey through the world of AI development, **www.nikhileshmishra.com** stands as your guiding star. This digital compass directs you to a constellation of resources, a compendium of platforms, libraries, and insights that illuminate your path. Here, you'll find recommendations that align with your goals, frameworks that resonate with your aspirations, and libraries that resonate with your projects. With each visit, you'll unveil a trove of knowledge, a symphony of guidance that steers you toward mastery. Let **www.nikhileshmishra.com** be your portal to enlightenment, your sanctuary of resources, and your forge of innovation.

The Forge of Creativity:

In the grand narrative of AI development platforms and libraries, innovation becomes a symphony of code and data, orchestrated by the tools that empower, streamline, and elevate. These platforms and libraries are not just tools; they are the conduits through which imagination flows, the bridges that connect the abstract to the tangible, and the sanctuaries where developers craft the future. With AI development platforms, novices become creators, and with AI libraries, challenges become solvable. Guided by the North Star of **www.nikhileshmishra.com**, you'll harness these tools to sculpt your ideas, shape your solutions, and contribute to the evolving tapestry of AI's impact on the world.

C. Collaborative AI research networks and conferences

In the boundless expanse of artificial intelligence, where the frontiers of knowledge are ever-expanding, collaborative AI research networks and conferences emerge as the nexus of innovation – the crossroads of minds, the crucibles of discovery, and the arenas where ideas evolve into breakthroughs. Envision a realm where researchers don't toil in isolation, but converge in symposia of intellect, where insights aren't hoarded, but shared with a symphony of camaraderie. This is the essence of collaborative AI research networks and conferences, where pixels on screens transform into portals of interaction, and auditoriums become theaters of enlightenment. As we delve into this realm of intellectual confluence, prepare to be captivated by the exchange of ideas, the incubation of knowledge, and the metamorphosis of insights into algorithms that shape the future. For further guidance and resources, let **www.nikhileshmishra.com** be your compass, pointing the way to this dynamic landscape of collaboration and innovation.

Collaborative AI Research Networks: Forging a Web of Expertise

Picture a global network where researchers, practitioners, and visionaries weave a web of expertise that spans continents and disciplines. Collaborative AI research networks are the digital arenas where minds intersect, where insights intersect, and where the symphony of knowledge reverberates through virtual corridors.

In these networks, researchers collaborate on projects, exchange findings, and elevate each other's work. The collective intellect transcends institutional boundaries, fusing diverse perspectives to tackle complex challenges. Here, novices find mentors, and experts find collaborators. Discussions unfold in virtual spaces, where threads of conversation weave the fabric of innovation. Collaborative AI research networks become the breeding grounds for breakthroughs, the cradles of creativity, and the incubators where research becomes a collaborative endeavor that transcends individual achievement.

Conferences: The Grand Stages of Intellectual Symphony

Imagine the grandeur of a conference hall, where minds gather like stars in a constellation, each emitting brilliance that enriches the galaxy of knowledge. Conferences are the grand stages where research is unveiled, insights are shared, and connections are forged. These gatherings become the arenas where the pulse of AI's evolution is felt, where trends are identified, and where the future is glimpsed.

Lectures by luminaries illuminate the paths of exploration, workshops delve into the intricacies of algorithms, and poster sessions showcase the visual symphonies of research findings. As attendees engage in conversations, debates, and knowledge exchanges, ideas collide and morph into new horizons of understanding. Conferences encapsulate the spirit of collaboration, shaping a future where the boundaries of AI knowledge are pushed and the horizons of innovation are expanded.

Guided by the North Star:

As you navigate the cosmos of collaborative AI research networks and conferences, let **www.nikhileshmishra.com** be your guiding star. This digital compass directs you to a constellation of resources, a trove of information, and a portal that unveils the schedule of conferences, provides insights into research networks, and offers recommendations to enhance your engagement. With each click, you'll embark on a journey that immerses you in the global symphony of AI collaboration. Let **www.nikhileshmishra.com** be your conduit to this realm of intellectual camaraderie, your sanctuary of resources, and your gateway to participation.

The Nexus of Progress:

In the grand narrative of collaborative AI research networks and conferences, innovation becomes a symphony conducted by the convergence of minds, where insights harmonize, and where breakthroughs resonate. These networks and conferences are not just events; they are the platforms that unite intellects, the marketplaces where ideas are bartered, and the sanctuaries where researchers weave the tapestry of AI's evolution. With collaborative AI research networks, minds converge; with conferences, ideas flourish. Guided by the North Star of **www.nikhileshmishra.com**, you'll navigate this landscape of intellectual interaction, amplifying your insights, expanding your horizons, and contributing to the ongoing symphony of AI's impact on the world.

CHAPTER 23

Building a Career in AI and ML

In the nebula of career possibilities, where aspirations converge with technology's constellations, building a career in AI and ML becomes a celestial journey of discovery, creation, and impact. Envision a trajectory where curiosity is your compass, algorithms are your compass, and innovation is your North Star. This is the essence of embarking on a career in AI and ML – a path that transcends job titles, a symphony of interdisciplinary knowledge, and a metamorphosis of roles that shape the digital landscapes of tomorrow. As you embark on this odyssey of intellect and ingenuity, prepare to be captivated by the fusion of curiosity and computation, the convergence of skill and strategy, and the transformation of aspirations into algorithms that shape the future.

A. Academic and industry career paths in AI

In the realm of artificial intelligence, where algorithms dance with data and creativity fuses with computation, two distinct but intertwined roads beckon aspiring minds – the academic path and the industrial path. These roads, though divergent in their destinations, converge in their pursuit of AI's boundless frontiers, each offering a unique tapestry of challenges, opportunities, and impact. Envision a journey where curiosity fuels innovation, where intellect meets application, and where the map to success is etched with algorithms and ingenuity. This is the essence of choosing between the academic and industrial career paths in AI – a choice that shapes not only your trajectory, but the trajectory of AI's evolution itself. As we embark on this exploration of possibilities, prepare to be captivated by the corridors of research and the landscapes of innovation, where the academic and industrial realms unfold as symphonies of mastery.

Academic Path: The Sanctum of Research and Discovery

Imagine the corridors of academia, where the pursuit of knowledge takes center stage, and the echoes of curiosity resonate through hallowed halls. The academic path in AI is a sanctuary for those who yearn to explore the uncharted territories of algorithms, push the boundaries of theory, and unravel the enigmas of intelligence.

Doctoral pursuits become odysseys of research, where novices become scholars, and scholars become architects of new paradigms. Here, you'll delve into the intricacies of machine learning, computational neuroscience, and natural language processing. Research projects become crucibles where ideas are forged, algorithms are birthed, and breakthroughs illuminate the path to AI's evolution. The academic path in AI is a symphony of exploration, where your mind becomes a vessel for the transmission of knowledge, and your insights become the building blocks of AI's future.

Industrial Path: The Forge of Innovation and Real-world Impact

In the bustling landscape of industry, AI takes on a dynamic role as the catalyst of innovation, the architect of solutions, and the harbinger of disruption. The industrial path in AI offers a realm where algorithms are sculpted into products, data becomes insight, and code transforms into tangible impact.

Within industrial domains, AI engineers and data scientists become the alchemists of algorithms, turning raw data into predictive models, crafting chatbots that anticipate needs, and orchestrating recommendation systems that enrich user experiences. This path presents a landscape where challenges become opportunities, where AI isn't just an academic exercise, but a toolkit for addressing real-world problems. The industrial path in AI is a symphony of innovation, where your code becomes a conduit for change, and your creations shape the products, services, and industries of tomorrow.

Convergence and Confluence: Guided by the North Star

As you stand at the crossroads of academic and industrial AI career paths, let your aspirations be guided by the North Star of your own passion, aptitude, and vision. While academia immerses you in the symphony of research, industrial domains invite you to compose the symphony of innovation. The convergence of both paths weaves a narrative of synergy, where academia informs industrial practices, and industry challenges stimulate academic inquiry. The tapestry of AI's impact is woven by those who embrace both paths, fostering a harmonious exchange between knowledge creation and real-world application.

For those seeking guidance on these divergent yet interconnected roads, **www.nikhileshmishra.com** becomes your North Star. It offers a constellation of insights, a trove of resources, and a beacon that illuminates the way, helping you navigate the labyrinthine choices of academia and industry in AI. With each step you take, whether within the hallowed halls of research or the dynamic corridors of industry, remember that your journey not only shapes your future but the destiny of AI itself – a destiny woven from the threads of innovation, mastery, and the unending quest for understanding in the universe of artificial intelligence.

B. Professional development and networking opportunities

In the cosmos of artificial intelligence, where innovation converges with imagination and algorithms interlace with aspirations, the path to excellence is not solitary. It's a symphony of collaboration, a confluence of expertise, and a dance of shared insights. Professional development and networking opportunities emerge as the constellations that guide ambitious minds through the nebulous expanse of AI, where careers are forged, knowledge is enriched, and horizons are expanded. Envision a journey where personal growth melds with collective progress, where connections become catalysts, and where each interaction weaves a thread in the tapestry of success. This is the essence of navigating the labyrinthine realm of AI through the lens of professional development and networking, where the pursuit of mastery becomes an art form guided by the North Star of continuous improvement.

Professional Development: Nurturing the Seeds of Mastery

Picture a garden where the seeds of potential are sown, carefully tended, and nurtured to bloom into a lush forest of expertise. Professional development in the realm of AI is the cultivator of these seeds, the orchestrator of growth, and the alchemist that transforms ambition into mastery.

Workshops become the crucibles where novices evolve into craftsmen, refining their skills in coding, data analysis, and algorithm design. Online courses unfurl like scrolls of knowledge, each lesson a step forward, each module an ascent toward mastery. Certifications become the badges of expertise, validating your proficiency in machine learning, neural networks, and AI ethics.

As you embark on this journey, remember that professional development isn't just a means to an end; it's a pilgrimage of perpetual growth. Each seminar, each certificate, and each hackathon shapes your intellectual landscape, transforming you into an architect of algorithms, a steward of data, and a sentinel of AI's evolution.

Networking: The Tapestry of Collective Wisdom

Imagine a grand hall where minds from diverse backgrounds converge, each conversation a thread that weaves the tapestry of collective wisdom. Networking in the AI universe is the loom upon which this tapestry is crafted, connecting individuals, domains, and perspectives into a harmonious symphony of collaboration.

Conferences become the amphitheaters of interaction, where scholars, practitioners, and visionaries gather to share insights, exchange ideas, and catalyze innovation. Meetups become the crucibles of camaraderie, where local communities of AI enthusiasts forge bonds that transcend pixels and screens. Online forums become the agora of discourse, where questions are posed, solutions are shared, and discussions spark the fire of collective understanding.

As you navigate this realm of networking, remember that every connection is a doorway to new perspectives, every conversation a wellspring of inspiration, and every collaboration a fusion of talents that propels the boundaries of AI's impact. The tapestry of AI's evolution is woven not just by algorithms but by the relationships, partnerships, and alliances that amplify the symphony of progress.

Guided by the North Star:

As you tread the path of professional development and networking in the AI cosmos, let the North Star of continuous improvement illuminate your way. **www.nikhileshmishra.com** becomes your guiding constellation, offering a treasure trove of resources, insights, and recommendations. It becomes your compass in the labyrinth of choices, your companion in the journey of growth, and your beacon in the quest for excellence.

Remember, in the grand narrative of AI's impact, your growth is the catalyst, your interactions are the catalysts, and your contributions are the harmonies that elevate the symphony of progress. Embrace professional development as the melody of your personal journey, and networking as the orchestration of collective brilliance. As you forge your path through the nebula of AI, may each step be a note of advancement, each connection a chord of collaboration, and each endeavor a crescendo of mastery.

C. Strategies for staying updated in a rapidly evolving field

In the dynamic realm of artificial intelligence, where

innovation streaks like comets and breakthroughs cascade like celestial waterfalls, staying updated is not a luxury – it's a necessity. As the tides of technology surge, and algorithms evolve with the speed of meteors, the quest to remain abreast becomes a symphony of vigilance, curiosity, and adaptability. Envision a voyage through the constellations of AI's evolution, where each shimmering star represents a strategy to keep you afloat in the ever-evolving sea of advancement. Prepare to embark on this celestial journey, guided by the North Star of continuous learning, with each strategy an instrument that resonates with the symphony of AI's progression.

Embrace Lifelong Learning: The Elixir of Relevance

Imagine a wellspring of knowledge that flows ceaselessly, a river of wisdom that never runs dry. Lifelong learning is the elixir that sustains your relevance in the rapidly evolving field of AI. Enroll in online courses, participate in workshops, and dive into tutorials that unveil the latest algorithms, methodologies, and tools. Lifelong learning transforms you into an avid explorer, charting the frontiers of AI with unquenchable curiosity.

Engage in Knowledge Communities: Echoes of Collective Wisdom

Visualize a bustling agora where minds converge, questions spark discussions, and insights ripple through the digital expanse. Knowledge communities, online forums, and social media groups are the echo chambers of collective wisdom. Engage in discussions, seek solutions to challenges, and share your insights. These communities become the amplifiers of your knowledge, the conduits of real-time updates, and the sounding boards for your ideas.

Follow Thought Leaders: The Beacons of Insight

Imagine a constellation of luminaries whose insights illuminate the darkness of uncertainty. Thought leaders, researchers, and industry experts are the beacons that guide your path. Follow their blogs, read their papers, and attend their talks. These thought leaders distill complex ideas into digestible insights, helping you navigate the complexity of AI's evolution.

Attend Conferences and Workshops: The Oases of Innovation

Envision a grand hall where innovation unfurls its wings, where ideas flow like rivers, and where connections become catalysts. Conferences and workshops are the oases where you quench your thirst for knowledge, forge collaborations, and witness the unveiling of breakthroughs. Attend events that resonate with your interests, and immerse yourself in the symphony of updates that reverberate through these gatherings.

Experiment and Apply: The Forge of Practical Wisdom

Picture a laboratory where hypotheses transform into insights, and algorithms are sculpted into solutions. Experiment with new techniques, apply cutting-edge methodologies to real-world challenges, and embark on projects that stretch your skills. Practical application not only hones your expertise but also deepens your understanding of AI's evolving landscape.

Embrace AI News and Blogs: The Chronicle of Progress

Imagine a digital library where AI's saga is chronicled in real-time. AI news portals, blogs, and newsletters become your chronicles of progress, delivering updates, insights, and analyses to your digital doorstep. Subscribe to reputable sources and stay informed about the latest breakthroughs, trends, and debates shaping the AI landscape.

Seek Mentorship and Collaboration: The Nexus of Experience

Envision a mentorship as a celestial alignment where experience intersects with curiosity, wisdom meets innovation, and guidance nurtures growth. Seek mentors whose expertise shines like guiding stars, and collaborate with peers whose diversity of skills enriches your perspective. Mentorship and collaboration become the nexus where wisdom converges, catalyzing your understanding and propelling your growth.

Guided by the North Star:

As you navigate the ever-evolving sea of AI, **www.nikhileshmishra.com** becomes your celestial map, guiding you to a constellation of resources, insights, and strategies. Let it be your North Star of guidance, helping you chart your course through the dynamic currents of progress. Remember, in the symphony of AI's evolution, staying updated isn't just a strategy; it's your ticket to becoming an architect of innovation, a sentinel of advancements, and a maestro who orchestrates the future. With each strategy you embrace, you forge a chord in the symphony, adding your voice to the resounding chorus of AI's transformative impact on the world.

Part VII

Interview Preparation

CHAPTER 24

Preparing for AI and ML Interviews

Embarking on a journey to conquer the realm of Artificial Intelligence and Machine Learning interviews is an exhilarating endeavor, one that requires strategic preparation and unwavering determination. In this pivotal chapter, we delve into the art of sculpting your mind into a fortress of knowledge and your skills into sharpened tools, all in pursuit of standing out in the dynamic landscape of interviews.

As you turn the pages ahead, you'll discover the blueprint for building your foundation – not just a rudimentary structure, but a robust stronghold. We'll unravel the secrets of honing your technical prowess, but beyond that, we'll explore the nuances of critical thinking, a skill coveted by the most discerning of interviewers. With practical insights and hands-on guidance, we'll navigate the treacherous waters of coding challenges and perplexing problem-solving scenarios.

But it's not just about answering questions; it's about crafting your unique narrative. Here, you'll learn to tell your story – of how you've journeyed through the intricacies of algorithms and data structures, of how you've tamed the complexity of machine learning models, and of how you've etched your mark on the tapestry of AI innovation.

So, ready your mind for an expedition into the realm of AI and ML interviews. Equip yourself with the tools, strategies, and insights that will not only help you conquer technical challenges but also allow you to shine as a poised and confident candidate. Let this chapter be your guiding light, illuminating your path toward mastering the art of preparing for AI and ML interviews.

A. Overview of AI and ML interview process

Embarking upon the journey of an AI and ML interview is akin to navigating uncharted territories, where each question posed and each challenge met is a chance to showcase your mettle in this ever-evolving realm. In this chapter, we unravel the multi-faceted tapestry of the AI and ML interview process, revealing the intricate layers that define success in this dynamic arena.

A Glimpse into the AI and ML Interview Landscape: Imagine stepping into a realm where algorithms dance, data whispers, and models sing with potential. The AI and ML interview process grants you entry into this realm, where your technical prowess, problem-solving finesse, and creative ingenuity are put to the test. Brace yourself for a curated symphony of inquiries that traverse the spectrum – from theory and application to coding acumen and architectural insight.

The Pinnacle of Technical Exploration: Prepare to be

enthralled by the labyrinthine mazes of algorithms, where classic dilemmas intertwine with avant-garde concepts. Your journey begins with a plunge into the depths of linear regression, where understanding nuances like regularization and bias-variance trade-offs becomes your guiding compass. Traverse the forests of decision trees and delve into the convolutional wonders of neural networks – a tour de force through supervised and unsupervised learning.

Coding Challenges

Cracking the Code of Success: Beyond theory lies the proving ground of coding challenges – an arena where algorithms and structures take tangible form. Here, the dance of logic and syntax takes center stage. Elevate your coding arsenal as you decipher enigmatic coding challenges, unraveling intricate problems with elegant solutions that mirror your analytical brilliance.

Crafting Thoughtful Responses

Beyond the Lines of Code: In the tapestry of an AI and ML interview, technical prowess is but one brushstroke. Delve into the art of explaining your thought process, dissecting intricate problems with eloquent clarity. Communicate how you navigate the complex currents of data analysis and model selection, showcasing your ability to transform the abstract into the comprehensible.

Navigating Real-world Scenarios: Taming the Wild Frontiers: Prepare to showcase your adaptability as you confront real-world scenarios that mirror the tumultuous challenges of the field. From handling noisy datasets to addressing ethical dilemmas, your voyage extends beyond the theoretical, demonstrating your capacity to wield AI and ML as tools for pragmatic problem-solving.

Conquering the Unseen Horizons: Mastering Behavioral and Soft Skills

While algorithms and data structures form the bedrock, behavioral prowess and soft skills paint the panorama. Ascend the summits of teamwork, empathy, and adaptability as you articulate how you thrive in collaborative environments, navigate evolving projects, and contribute to the ever-shifting tapestry of AI innovation.

In the realm of AI and ML interviews, each interaction is a canvas upon which your potential is painted. Armed with this comprehensive overview, you embark on your odyssey – where the alchemy of technical brilliance and human connection fashions the masterpiece that is your interview performance. As you progress through this chapter, remember that while AI and ML are the tools, you are the artisan, crafting a narrative that resonates with interviewers and propels you toward success in this captivating voyage of discovery.

B. Building a strong foundation in key concepts

The foundation upon which the towering edifices of AI and ML rest is not merely a bedrock; it is an intricate tapestry woven with the threads of knowledge, understanding, and intellectual acumen. In this chapter, we embark upon a voyage of enlightenment, excavating the bedrock of fundamental concepts that underpin the grand architecture of artificial intelligence and machine learning.

Unearthing the Cornerstones

Picture yourself as an intrepid explorer, armed with the tools of curiosity and intellectual hunger. As you delve into the depths of AI and ML, you unearth the cornerstones of mathematical and statistical principles – the very keystones upon which the algorithms and models stand. Traverse the terrain of linear algebra, where vectors and matrices intertwine, and probability theory, where randomness and uncertainty become your companions.

A Symphony of Algorithms and Models

Amidst the cacophony of algorithms and models, clarity is your guiding light. Immerse yourself in the harmonious symphony of regression and classification, as linear and logistic regression emerge as the overture. Progress to the crescendo of decision trees, where the branches of possibility flourish, and allow the resonating echoes of support vector machines to captivate your senses.

The Ethereal Universe of Neural Networks

Venture deeper, into the ethereal universe of neural networks, where neurons ignite and connections propagate. Absorb the elegance of convolutional neural networks, where images transform into patterns, and embrace the cadence of recurrent neural networks, where sequences are unraveled.

Beyond Algorithms: The Soul of Data

As you mold your foundation, remember that data is the lifeblood coursing through the veins of AI and ML. Glean insights into data preprocessing – the art of cleansing, transforming, and augmenting raw data into gems of intelligence. From dimensionality reduction to feature engineering, you become an alchemist, distilling the essence of information.

A Toolkit of Tools and Libraries

Amidst the conceptual expanse, a toolkit awaits – tools and libraries that breathe life into abstractions. Embrace Python's symphony of syntax, wield libraries like NumPy and pandas as your brushes, and let scikit-learn be your artist's palette. With every code snippet, you orchestrate the symphony of AI and ML concepts into a tangible reality.

The Quest for Continuous Learning

But the foundation is not static; it evolves with the tide of innovation. In this ever-transforming landscape, be prepared for a lifelong journey of learning. Let curiosity be your compass, and the pursuit of mastery, your lodestar.

In this chapter, you're not merely building a foundation – you're forging a legacy. As you absorb the intricacies of mathematical principles, algorithms, models, and tools, remember that this is the bedrock upon which you'll stand, the launchpad from which you'll ascend to ever-greater heights. With each concept you grasp, you sculpt your own path within the realm of AI and ML, and with each formula you internalize, you imbue your journey with the power to innovate, create, and transform.

C. Practicing coding and problem-solving skills

In the realm of artificial intelligence and machine learning, the mind is not merely a vessel; it is a crucible where raw curiosity transmutes into ingenious solutions. In this chapter, we traverse the labyrinth of coding and problem-solving, where the crucible of your intellect refines your abilities into the sharpest of tools.

The Forge of Logic and Creativity

Imagine yourself as an artisan, crafting intricate mechanisms from the raw materials of logic and creativity. Coding and problem-solving become your forge, and each challenge you encounter is an opportunity to mold and temper your skills. Like a master blacksmith, you learn to wield algorithms and data structures, shaping them into elegant solutions that stand the test of complexity.

The Puzzle of Algorithms

Envision each algorithm as a puzzle piece – a distinctive shape that fits into the grand mosaic of problem-solving. You venture into the landscape of sorting and searching, traversing graphs, and conquering dynamic programming. As you assemble these pieces, the bigger picture emerges – a rich tapestry of computational elegance designed to crack the enigma of real-world challenges.

Sculpting with Data Structures

In the crucible, data structures are your chisels, allowing you to sculpt ideas into functional creations. Explore the landscape of arrays, linked lists, stacks, and queues. Let trees and graphs become the mediums through which you express your ingenuity. As you manipulate these structures, you not only solve problems but also cultivate the art of optimizing, refactoring, and transforming complexity into elegance.

From LeetCode to Real-World Complexities

The crucible extends beyond theoretical domains. Platforms

like LeetCode, HackerRank, and Codeforces offer not just challenges but arenas for growth. Like a gladiator, you pit your intellect against an array of problems, developing the acumen to dissect complex issues and formulate elegant solutions. Yet, remember that the ultimate prize is not just a solution; it's the mastery of translating coding prowess into real-world impact.

Cultivating Problem-Solving Intuition

Beyond syntax and structure lies the elusive realm of intuition – the ability to approach problems with strategic foresight. As you navigate coding challenges, you cultivate the intuition to discern patterns, deconstruct roadblocks, and forge pathways to success. This intuition becomes a compass guiding you through the uncharted territories of problem-solving.

Collaboration and Peer Learning

The crucible is not a solitary space; it's a forge where collaboration tempers your skills. Engage in pair programming, code reviews, and hackathons. These interactions become the bellows that fan the flames of your intellect, exposing you to diverse perspectives and expanding your problem-solving toolkit.

The Ever-Burning Flame of Learning

Consider the crucible not as a static furnace, but as an ever-burning flame that fuels your passion for learning. The journey of coding and problem-solving is a perpetual quest, where each challenge conquered becomes a stepping stone to the next enigma. Stay open to experimentation, embrace failure as a teacher, and let the process of refinement kindle your pursuit of excellence.

In this chapter, the crucible of coding and problem-solving becomes the forge where raw aptitude fuses with strategic finesse. As you immerse yourself in this realm, remember that each line of code, each algorithm mastered, is not just a technical accomplishment – it's a testament to your capacity to unravel complexity, innovate, and create solutions that reshape the contours of possibility.

CHAPTER 25

Common Interview Questions and Answers

Imagine standing at the threshold of opportunity, where questions become pathways to showcasing your brilliance and insights. In this chapter, we step into the realm of common interview questions and answers – a symphony of inquiry and response that orchestrates your narrative in the grand performance of an AI and ML interview.

The Stage of Inquiry

Envision each question as a spotlight illuminating a fragment of your expertise, inviting you to narrate your journey through the landscape of AI and ML. Here, theory and practice intertwine, as algorithms transform into anecdotes and models manifest as solutions. The stage is set for you to articulate your passion, knowledge, and strategic finesse.

Navigating the Maze of Curiosity

Picture yourself as a cartographer, charting your path through the maze of questions that span the AI and ML cosmos. As each question unfurls, you become an intrepid explorer, revealing how you decipher the enigma of overfitting, how you optimize model performance, and how you navigate the intricate labyrinth of bias and fairness.

A Tapestry of Articulation

Beyond technical proficiency lies the art of articulation – the symphony of language and logic. With eloquence, you elucidate your thoughts, crafting a narrative that transcends code. As you respond to questions about model evaluation, feature engineering, and neural network intricacies, you weave a tapestry that showcases your cognitive prowess.

Deconstructing Complexity

Each question is a portal to deconstructing complexity into comprehensible threads. Dive into the depths of gradient descent, peeling away layers to reveal how you tame the optimization landscape. Elaborate on your mastery of regularization, unmasking how you strike the balance between bias and variance. With every answer, you unfold the secrets of your analytical prowess.

Coding and Conundrums

Coding questions become a canvas, where you paint elegant solutions with the brushstrokes of your syntax. From traversing binary trees to implementing dynamic programming, you exhibit your coding finesse. As you unravel each challenge, you illuminate your ability to translate logic into code, revealing your prowess beyond theoretical musings.

The Choreography of Behavioral Insights: In this symphony, it's not just algorithms that dance; it's your behavior, your disposition, and your collaborative spirit. When questions delve into your teamwork acumen, your approach to challenging scenarios, and your ethical compass, you choreograph a performance that embodies the holistic essence of your candidacy.

Crafting Your Narrative

Each answer is a chapter in your narrative, an opportunity to showcase your unique perspective and journey. You narrate how you decipher data's cryptic messages, sculpting insights that drive decision-making. You recount the symphony of algorithms and models, underscoring your ability to orchestrate intelligence from complexity.

As you journey through the realm of common interview questions and answers, remember that you are not just answering inquiries – you are crafting a story. With every response, you shape your identity as an AI and ML practitioner, a seeker of knowledge, and a master of innovation. Let each answer resonate like a melodious note, harmonizing your expertise with the symphony of possibility that is an AI and ML interview.

A. Supervised and unsupervised learning questions

In the realm of artificial intelligence and machine learning, the duality of supervised and unsupervised learning is more than just a classification; it's a symphony of methodologies that harmonize to reveal the secrets encoded within data. In this chapter, we embark on a journey through a labyrinth of questions, exploring the depths of supervised and unsupervised learning with a quest for understanding that is both profound and illuminating.

Supervised Learning: Unveiling Patterns in Data's Tapestry

Imagine data as a richly woven tapestry, each thread a data point and each hue a potential insight. Supervised learning, the weaver's hand, strives to unravel the patterns entwined within. As you navigate this landscape, envision regression as a painter's brush, capturing the continuum of relationships. Embrace classification as the conductor of a harmonious symphony, orchestrating data into distinct categories.

The Interplay of Features and Labels

Within the realm of supervised learning, each question about features and labels serves as a thread that binds data's narrative. Explore the artistry of feature engineering, where you mold raw attributes into beacons of intelligence. Delve into label encoding and one-hot encoding, deciphering the symphony of data transformation that fuels algorithmic interpretation.

Navigating Overfitting and Bias: Striking the Balance

As you unravel the fabric of supervised learning, you encounter the specters of overfitting and bias. With the brush of regularization, you temper models to strike a harmonious balance between complexity and generalization. Navigate the delicate terrain of bias-variance trade-off, a dance of precision and adaptability that shapes the very core of your predictive prowess.

Unsupervised Learning: The Uncharted Territories of Insight

Step beyond the realm of labeled data, and you enter the realm of unsupervised learning – a terra incognita of exploration. Imagine clustering as a cartographer's quill, delineating territories within data's expanse. Picture dimensionality reduction as a sculptor's chisel, revealing the latent essence of information beneath the surface.

The Symphony of Clustering: Groups and Anomalies

Dive deep into clustering, where data points find their kindred spirits, and groups emerge like constellations in the night sky. Embrace K-means as a cosmic ballet, arranging data into harmonious ensembles. Uncover hierarchical clustering as an architect, sculpting dendrograms that illustrate relationships etched in data's essence.

The Elegance of Dimensionality Reduction

As you embark on the journey of dimensionality reduction, envision data as a multidimensional canvas. Enter Principal Component Analysis (PCA), a maestro that conducts the reductionist symphony, revealing the most salient notes. Traverse t-SNE as a traveler of the manifold, navigating the intricate terrain of high-dimensional spaces.

Anomaly Detection: Unveiling the Extraordinary

In this landscape, anomaly detection is your lantern, illuminating the extraordinary within the ordinary. Imagine data as a tapestry interwoven with hidden threads of peculiarity. With every Isolation Forest and Local Outlier Factor, you embark on a quest to unearth anomalies, exposing the unique notes that resonate within data's composition.

Building a Toolbox of Understanding

As you explore the tapestry of supervised and unsupervised learning, remember that these methodologies are not just tools; they're lenses through which you perceive the world hidden within data. Each question posed, each answer discovered, enriches your toolbox of understanding. With every insight, you gain the ability to orchestrate intelligence from complexity, revealing the symphony of knowledge that underscores your mastery.

B. Model evaluation and optimization techniques

In the grand theater of artificial intelligence and machine learning, models are the protagonists, and their performance is the crescendo that resonates with insight and innovation. In this chapter, we unveil the artistry of model evaluation and optimization – a symphony of metrics, techniques, and strategies that elevate your models to the pinnacle of predictive prowess.

The Overture of Model Evaluation: Metrics that Echo Insight

Imagine each model as a composer's opus, each note a prediction, and each chord a decision. Model evaluation becomes the conductor's baton, guiding your symphony to resounding success. Engage with metrics that dance between precision and recall, accuracy and F1-score, ROC curves and AUC – each a nuanced brushstroke on the canvas of model performance.

Precision and Recall: Balancing Act of Impact

Within the realm of evaluation, envision precision as a scalpel that cleaves truth from prediction, while recall is a net that captures all that's true. With these tools, you sculpt models that navigate the fine line between identifying positives and minimizing false positives. This balance becomes your artistry, amplifying the impact of your predictions.

Accuracy and Misclassification: The Symphony of Correctness

As you traverse the landscape of accuracy, imagine your model as a virtuoso performing an intricate piece. Accuracy becomes the melody of correctness, resonating with harmonious proportions. Delve into misclassification matrices, where you dissect errors with surgical precision, unraveling the nuances of false positives and false negatives.

AUC and ROC: The Cadence of Model Performance

Picture your model's journey as a dance upon the Receiver Operating Characteristic (ROC) curve, each step reflecting sensitivity and specificity. Envision Area Under the Curve (AUC) as the crescendo that measures your model's discriminative ability. Here, the curve becomes a dance partner, guiding your steps toward optimal model design.

Optimization: The Alchemy of Model Mastery

Optimization is not merely a process; it's the alchemical fusion of insight, experimentation, and refinement. Imagine hyperparameters as elements in a cosmic brew, where learning rates and regularization coefficients meld into a recipe for performance. Engage in grid and random search, visualizing the evolution of your models as they journey through parameter space.

Cross-Validation: Weaving the Fabric of Reliability

Within the tapestry of optimization, cross-validation is your loom, weaving threads of reliability into the fabric of model assessment. Envision k-folds as the warp that provides stability, while metrics like Mean Squared Error and Root Mean Squared Error measure the weft of performance. The resulting tapestry is a testament to the robustness of your models.

Bias and Variance: The Balancing Act of Generalization

In the realm of optimization, bias and variance are your scales, tipping the balance between underfitting and overfitting. Imagine bias as the anchor that stabilizes your model's grasp on truth, and variance as the kite that soars into the realms of complexity. Here, the equilibrium of model design becomes your mandate – a mastery of predictive equilibrium.

Ensemble Techniques: The Harmony of Aggregation

Imagine models as instruments in an ensemble, each contributing a unique timbre to the symphony of predictions. Embrace bagging and boosting as your maestros, orchestrating a harmonious symphony of aggregated models. With Random Forests, envision a grand orchestra where each decision tree harmonizes to create a robust, predictive crescendo.

In the journey of model evaluation and optimization, you are both conductor and composer. Each question posed, each technique embraced, refines your ability to harness the power of models, transforming raw data into orchestrated intelligence. As you wield metrics and strategies with artistry, remember that you are not just optimizing models; you are sculpting instruments of insight that resonate with the symphony of innovation in the ever-evolving realm of AI and ML.

C. Deep learning and neural network concepts

In the labyrinth of artificial intelligence, deep learning emerges as a luminary – a beacon that illuminates the realms of complexity and unlocks the vaults of intelligence. In this chapter, we embark on a voyage through the cosmos of deep learning and neural network concepts, where neurons ignite, layers intertwine, and intelligence unfurls in the symphony of data.

The Symphony of Neurons: Orchestrating Intelligence

Imagine neurons as the virtuosos of deep learning, each synapse a note, and each layer a harmony. Deep within neural networks, these neurons ignite with energy, traversing pathways of information, decoding data's melodies. As you journey through this symphony, understand how neurons synthesize knowledge, amplifying their intensity with each iteration.

Feedforward and Backpropagation: The Ballet of Learning

Visualize feedforward propagation as a dance of data, where inputs waltz through layers, transformed by weights and biases. In contrast, backpropagation becomes a graceful encore, as errors flow backward, refining each weight for optimal performance. This ballet of learning captures the essence of neural networks – a harmonious interplay of input and adaptation.

Convolutional Elegance: Crafting Visual Perception

Step into the canvas of convolutional neural networks (CNNs), where pixels metamorphose into patterns, and images evolve into understanding. Envision convolutional layers as brushes, capturing local features, and pooling layers as sculptors, chiseling intricacies. With CNNs, you paint a portrait of visual perception, decoding the language of images.

Sequences and Recurrence: Echoes of Temporal Understanding

In the tapestry of deep learning, recurrent neural networks (RNNs) become the weavers of time, unraveling sequential insight. Imagine each cell as a stanza, and the hidden state as the rhythm that carries memory. From sentiment analysis to machine translation, RNNs infuse your understanding with the cadence of context.

LSTM and GRU: Architectural Sonnets of Memory

Within RNNs, envision Long Short-Term Memory (LSTM) cells as poetic sonnets of memory, capturing long-range dependencies. Gaze upon Gated Recurrent Units (GRUs) as structured quatrains, simplifying complexity while preserving depth. These architectural gems enrich your neural network repertoire, amplifying your mastery of sequential intelligence.

Generative Splendor: From Dreams to Realities

Step into the realm of generative models, where dreams transmute into realities. GANs (Generative Adversarial Networks) become the maestros of creation, orchestrating duels between generator and discriminator. Imagine the generator as an artist, crafting images, text, and music, while the discriminator acts as the discerning critic, shaping artistry through feedback.

Transfer Learning: Adapting Knowledge, Amplifying Potential

Visualize transfer learning as a library of wisdom, where knowledge acquired from one task enriches another. Conceive of pre-trained models as volumes of expertise, ready to be adapted and fine-tuned. With transfer learning, you become an architect of adaptation, constructing bridges that amplify your neural network's potential.

The Symphony Continues: Lifelong Learning and Innovation

In the symphony of deep learning and neural network concepts, remember that you are not merely a listener; you are a conductor, a composer. Each concept embraced, each layer decoded, contributes to a symphony that evolves beyond the boundaries of today. As you navigate the complexities, innovate with architecture, and push the boundaries of possibility, you contribute to a crescendo that resonates with the infinite potential of AI's harmonious future.

CHAPTER 26

Case Studies and Real-world Scenarios

Step beyond the realm of abstraction, for in the hallowed halls of case studies and real-world scenarios, artificial intelligence and machine learning unfurl their wings to touch the tapestry of reality. In this chapter, we embark on a journey that transcends the theoretical, immersing ourselves in the vivid landscapes where AI's transformative magic weaves seamlessly into the fabric of our world.

The Theater of Applied Intelligence

Imagine the stage set, not in the confines of code or algorithms, but on the grand theater of real-world challenges. Here, AI and ML take center stage as protagonists, unraveling dilemmas, illuminating possibilities, and crafting solutions that breathe life into data's narrative. This is the theater of applied intelligence, where case studies unveil the artistry of problem-solving and innovation.

From Pixels to Precision: Healthcare's Diagnostic Symphony

Envision medical imaging as a symphony of pixels, where each hue tells a story of health or ailment. In this tableau, AI becomes the virtuoso, decoding images with the precision of a maestro's baton. Explore how convolutional neural networks (CNNs) navigate the landscape of radiology, discerning the subtleties of disease and anomaly. Through case studies, witness how AI illuminates the path to timely diagnoses, and how pixels evolve into portraits of hope.

Financial Algorithms: Charting a Symphony of Predictions

Imagine the stock market as a symphony, each rise and fall a note in the score of financial dynamics. Here, AI dons the role of composer, orchestrating algorithms that predict and adapt to market movements. Dive into case studies where recurrent neural networks (RNNs) decode the rhythm of financial data, and ensemble techniques harmonize predictions. Witness how AI transforms complexity into insight, allowing investors to dance to the tune of informed decisions.

Cognitive Navigators: Autonomous Vehicles' Epic Odyssey

Picture a world where roads become neural pathways, and cars become cognitive navigators, adept at understanding and responding to their environment. Autonomous vehicles are not just machines; they are orchestras of AI, conducting symphonies of perception, planning, and control. Journey through case studies where sensor fusion becomes a sonata, and reinforcement learning steers vehicles through complex terrains. Witness the harmonious interplay of sensors and algorithms, where safety and innovation intertwine.

Language's Luminous Evolution: Chatbots and Customer Experience

In the realm of customer experience, imagine conversations as a ballet of words, where chatbots become the dancers, twirling through the nuances of language. Witness how natural language processing (NLP) morphs into a vibrant tapestry of interaction, as case studies unveil chatbots that converse seamlessly across languages and contexts. Explore how sentiment analysis becomes the conductor, tuning customer interactions to the symphony of satisfaction.

The Compass of Exploration: Unraveling Uncharted Territories

As we delve into case studies and real-world scenarios, we navigate not just the known, but the uncharted territories of innovation. These studies are our compass, guiding us through the seas of uncertainty and complexity. With each case dissected, each scenario explored, we unlock insights that not only enrich our understanding but also shape the future landscape of AI and ML applications.

In this chapter, the case studies and real-world scenarios become our windows to AI's transformative power. They bridge the gap between theory and application, revealing how the symphony of algorithms harmonizes with the cadence of reality. With each case, we not only unravel solutions but also sow seeds of inspiration, reminding us that AI and ML are not mere tools, but conduits that orchestrate the symphony of progress in the ever-evolving tapestry of human ingenuity.

A. Solving complex AI and ML problems

In the realm of artificial intelligence and machine learning, complexity is not a challenge to shy away from; it's an invitation to unleash the full spectrum of your cognitive prowess. In this chapter, we embark on a journey that delves into the intricacies of solving complex AI and ML problems – a symphony of analytical finesse, innovative thinking, and strategic mastery that unveils the art of unraveling enigmas.

Deciphering Complexity: The Mosaic of Challenge

Imagine complex problems as mosaics, each piece a data point, and each hue a dimension of understanding. Your role is that of an interpreter, deciphering the language of complexity. As you approach these puzzles, envision yourself as a detective, following the trail of data breadcrumbs, seeking patterns amidst the labyrinthine intricacies.

The Architecture of Problem Framing: Before embarking on the journey of solving, one must forge a roadmap. Think of problem framing as the architectural blueprint – a foundation upon which solutions are erected. In this phase, you sculpt the problem's dimensions, identifying inputs, outputs, and variables. Like an architect, you lay the groundwork, ensuring clarity and alignment before the construction of solutions begins.

Feature Engineering: The Alchemy of Data Transformation

Visualize feature engineering as alchemy, transforming raw data into the gold of insights. Each feature is a note in the symphony, and your role is that of a composer, orchestrating attributes that resonate with predictive power. Craft features that capture the essence of the problem, harmonizing data's nuances into a melody of intelligence.

Model Selection: The Artistry of Algorithmic Choice

Within the arsenal of AI and ML, algorithms are your brushes, each one leaving a unique stroke on the canvas of prediction. Embrace model selection as an artistry of choice – a decision that hinges on the problem's nature, data volume, and desired outcomes. Imagine Random Forests as the lush strokes of a landscape painter, while Support Vector Machines are the precise etchings of a portrait artist.

Ensemble Mastery: The Symphony of Fusion

Ensemble techniques become your symphony conductor, orchestrating models into harmonious crescendos. Think of ensembles as a masterful fusion, combining the brilliance of individual models into a unified prediction. Embrace bagging and boosting as your musical notes, blending models' strengths into a symphony of heightened accuracy and robustness.

Hyperparameter Tuning: The Refinement Ballet

Imagine hyperparameters as dancers, each step a configuration that influences your model's performance. Hyperparameter tuning becomes a ballet of refinement, where you choreograph the dance of learning rates, regularization strengths, and batch sizes. With each iteration, you refine your model's choreography, elevating its performance to the crescendo of optimal precision.

A Mindful Approach to Evaluation: Metrics as Compass Points

Think of model evaluation as a compass, guiding you through the labyrinth of complexity. Metrics become your true north, steering your efforts towards performance measurement. Envision metrics as constellations, illuminating the path of success. Traverse the terrain of precision and recall, F1-score and AUC, understanding each metric's unique role in your analytical voyage.

Innovation through Iteration: The Symphony of Learning

Solving complex AI and ML problems is not a linear path; it's a symphony of iteration and innovation. Imagine each attempt as a note, each iteration as a movement. Embrace failure as a prelude to success, as each misstep becomes a learning opportunity. Like a composer refining a symphony, you iterate, adapt, and evolve until your solution resonates with the harmony of insight.

In this chapter, complexity becomes your canvas, and your expertise is the brush that unveils its mysteries. As you unravel complex AI and ML problems, remember that you are not just a solver; you are an architect of innovation, a conductor of insights. With every challenge embraced, every solution crafted, you contribute to the symphony of human intelligence, painting the world with the hues of progress and possibility.

B. Working with messy or unstructured data

In the realm of artificial intelligence and machine learning, data is the raw material from which intelligence blossoms. Yet, not all data arrives pristine and organized; some emerge as chaotic symphonies, where notes scatter and patterns elude. In this chapter, we embark on a journey that embraces the art of working with messy or unstructured data – a dance of transformation, where chaos metamorphoses into clarity.

The Chaos of Unstructured Data: A Symphony Untamed

Imagine unstructured data as a symphony untamed, where notes of information disperse, and melodies of meaning elude casual observation. Your role is that of a conductor, orchestrating a transformative symphony that brings coherence to the cacophony. As you embrace messy data, envision yourself as a virtuoso, wielding techniques that decipher, discern, and distill.

Data Preprocessing: The Art of Refinement

Like a sculptor chiseling a masterpiece from a block of marble, data preprocessing becomes your refining process. Visualize cleaning as polishing, where you scrub away noise, inconsistencies, and redundancies. Think of transformation as sculpting, molding raw attributes into insightful features. Embrace normalization and scaling as harmonizing tools, ensuring each attribute resonates with data's true essence.

Natural Language Processing: Conversing with Textual Chaos

Envision text data as a linguistic riddle, where words interlace and meaning is woven. In this realm, natural language processing (NLP) becomes your lexicon, enabling conversations with text. Imagine tokenization as an interpreter, dissecting sentences into words. See stemming and lemmatization as linguists, simplifying variations. As you dance through NLP, text's chaos converges into conversations of intelligence.

Image Analysis: Extracting Essence from Pixels

Think of images as visual enigmas, where pixels blend into intricate compositions. Image analysis becomes your visual interpreter, discerning features, patterns, and significance. Imagine convolutional neural networks (CNNs) as the visionaries, capturing local details through filters. Embrace image augmentation as a palette, enriching your understanding through transformations. In this realm, pixels metamorphose into the poetry of insight.

Feature Engineering: A Symphony of Meaningful Attributes

In the realm of messy data, feature engineering becomes your symphony of meaning. Visualize features as musical notes, each one contributing to the symphony's harmony. Feature extraction becomes a composer's craft, harmonizing attributes into patterns. Dimensionality reduction becomes your conductor's baton, ensuring that only the most salient notes grace the score.

Outlier Detection: Illuminating Shadows of Anomaly

Imagine outliers as shadows that obscure the truth within data's light. Outlier detection becomes your lantern, illuminating these shadows, revealing anomalies that hold the keys to understanding.

Visualize isolation forests as the sentinels, identifying data points that deviate from the norm. Envision clustering as a spotlight, bringing anomalies center stage for exploration.

Time Series Analysis: Unraveling Temporal Threads

Picture time series data as threads of time woven into intricate patterns. Time series analysis becomes your loom, unravelling temporal insights. Imagine autoregressive integrated moving average (ARIMA) models as weavers, forecasting trends through historical threads. Visualize long short-term memory (LSTM) networks as the storytellers, navigating sequential data's labyrinth.

Embracing the Symphony of Transformation: As you work with messy or unstructured data, remember that you are not just a data scientist; you are an artist, transforming chaos into clarity. Each technique you wield, each insight you glean, contributes to a symphony of transformation. In the realm of AI and ML, the artistry of working with unstructured data is a testament to your ability to tame complexity, conducting a symphony that resonates with the melody of insight.

C. Handling trade-offs and ethical considerations

In the intricate tapestry of artificial intelligence and machine learning, every decision is a brushstroke that shapes the canvas of progress. Yet, as we tread this path of innovation, we encounter trade-offs and ethical crossroads that demand not just technical finesse, but also a profound understanding of the human impact. In this chapter, we navigate the delicate dance of handling trade-offs and ethical considerations – a symphony of choices that harmonize technology's potential with humanity's values.

The Balancing Act of Trade-offs: A Mosaic of Choices

Imagine each trade-off as a mosaic, where each tile represents a decision that influences the bigger picture. Just as a painter selects hues that evoke emotion, you, too, are a creator, crafting choices that balance accuracy and simplicity, computation and time. Picture yourself as an architect, erecting bridges between conflicting priorities, ensuring that each trade-off resonates with the symphony of purpose.

Performance vs. Interpretability: The Duet of Understanding

Envision performance as a soaring melody, where complex models scale the heights of predictive power. Yet, beneath this melody lies the bassline of interpretability – the understanding that guides decisions. Like a duet, performance and interpretability harmonize. As you choose between complex deep learning architectures and interpretable models, remember that understanding is the compass that guides users through the landscape of insights.

Bias vs. Fairness: Crafting Equal Melodies

In the realm of data, imagine bias as a discordant note that skews models' harmony. Fairness becomes your conductor's wand, ensuring that each prediction is free from the taint of prejudice. Think of bias mitigation as a counter-melody, harmonizing with the main theme of predictive accuracy. In this symphony of ethics, fairness is your compass, guiding you towards compositions that echo with equal melodies for all.

Data Privacy vs. Innovation: A Serenade of Trust

Visualize data privacy as a sonata of trust, where users' sensitive information finds refuge in secure architectures. Innovation becomes your composer's pen, inscribing solutions that push boundaries. Consider federated learning as the symphony of privacy and innovation, where models learn without compromising data integrity. As you dance between the dueling motifs of privacy and progress, remember that trust is the timbre that resonates through the symphony of user empowerment.

Utility vs. Security: The Rhapsody of Protection

Imagine utility as a rhapsody of functionality, where AI-driven conveniences unfurl like a musical cascade. Yet, the shadows of security loom, casting the question of protection. Encryption becomes your harmonizing thread, weaving utility with layers of safety. Like a composer crafting a crescendo, you harmonize utility with security, ensuring that each innovation is underpinned by a fortress of protection.

Economic Impact vs. Employment: An Overture of Adaptation

Envision the economic impact of automation as an overture of transformation, where industries evolve and landscapes shift. Employment's chorus raises the question of adaptation. Consider reskilling initiatives as the theme of continuity, ensuring that advancements are accompanied by opportunities. Like a conductor leading an orchestra, you conduct the symphony of economic impact and employment, harmonizing progress with inclusivity.

The Moral Melody: Harmony with Human Values

In the complex symphony of trade-offs and ethical considerations, remember that each choice resonates with a moral melody. The compass that guides your decisions is not just technical proficiency; it's the alignment with human values. As you weigh trade-offs and navigate ethical landscapes, remember that you are not just a technologist; you are a guardian of innovation's impact. The symphony you conduct is one of harmonizing progress with the cadence of human dignity, crafting a narrative where AI and ML innovations are compositions that enrich lives, uplift societies, and echo the harmony of our collective values.

Part VIII

Guidance for Interviewers

CHAPTER 27

Conducting Effective AI and ML Interviews

In the realm where algorithms unfurl the tapestry of intelligence, and data whispers its tales of insights, conducting interviews for artificial intelligence and machine learning becomes a symphony of discovery and evaluation. Imagine stepping into an auditorium of intellect, where candidates become the notes that harmonize with the chords of innovation. In this chapter, we embark on a journey to master the art of conducting effective AI and ML interviews – a virtuoso's pursuit that seeks not just technical prowess, but the resonance of potential and passion.

The Auditorium of Insight: Where Minds Converge

Visualize the interview process as an auditorium of insight, where minds converge to unveil the symphony of knowledge. Like a conductor, you stand at the helm, orchestrating interactions that illuminate technical brilliance and ingenuity. As you enter this space, envision yourself as a curator, nurturing an environment where expertise resonates and passion flourishes.

Crafting the Prelude: Setting the Stage for Success

Before the interview unfolds, imagine crafting the prelude – the stage upon which candidates' talents shine. Like a playwright, you design questions that unfold the narrative of skills and potential. Think of coding assessments as the overture, where algorithms and logic begin their melodious dance. This is your canvas, and each question is a brushstroke that paints a portrait of expertise.

Understanding the Ensemble of Skillsets

Envision skillsets as instruments in an ensemble, each one contributing to the symphony of AI and ML proficiency. As you delve into technical aspects, picture yourself as a composer, discerning the harmonies of programming languages, data manipulation, and algorithmic reasoning. From Python's melodies to SQL's chords, you explore how each skill complements the symphony.

Probing with Precision: Questioning Techniques as Refrains

Think of questioning techniques as refrains that guide the interview's tempo and depth. Imagine behavioral questions as lyrical explorations of candidates' experiences, shedding light on collaboration, adaptability, and problem-solving. Technical questions become the rhythm section, measuring expertise in model selection, evaluation, and optimization. As you probe, remember that each refrain reveals a facet of the candidate's symphony.

Collaborative Crescendo: Assessing Team Dynamics

Envision collaborative skills as a crescendo, where candidates harmonize with colleagues in the symphony of teamwork. Imagine scenario-based questions as duets, exploring how candidates contribute to AI and ML orchestras. As you evaluate how well they synchronize, picture yourself as a conductor, observing how their notes blend with the ensemble, creating a harmonious impact.

Unveiling the Motif of Problem Solving: Algorithmic Elegance

Picture problem-solving as a motif, woven into the fabric of AI and ML expertise. As you delve into algorithmic questions, envision yourself as a virtuoso, deciphering candidates' thought processes like the nuances of a musical score. From decision trees to gradient descent, you explore how elegantly they compose solutions that harmonize with complexity.

Assessing the Melody of Innovation: Project and Experience Evaluation

Imagine projects and experience as melodies composed by candidates' ingenuity. Picture yourself as a music critic, assessing the melodies they've orchestrated in the past. Delve into their symphonies of innovation – from image recognition to natural language processing – and evaluate how their notes have shaped the landscape of AI and ML.

The Encore of Potential and Passion: Gauging Curiosity and Learning

Envision potential and passion as the encore that lingers long after the interview's final note. Think of curiosity as a melody that lingers in the air, transcending the boundaries of technical knowledge. Visualize your role as a mentor, gauging candidates' appetite for learning, their enthusiasm to explore uncharted territories, and their dedication to the lifelong symphony of growth.

In this chapter, conducting effective AI and ML interviews becomes a journey of orchestration, where each question, each interaction, is a note in the symphony of assessment. As you guide candidates through this virtuoso's pursuit, remember that you are not just an interviewer; you are a curator of talent, a conductor of potential, and a guardian of the symphony of AI and ML excellence.

A. Structuring interview questions for various roles

In the grand tapestry of artificial intelligence and machine learning, interview questions are the threads that weave candidates' expertise into the fabric of innovation. Just as a composer meticulously arranges notes to craft a symphony, structuring interview questions for various roles becomes a composition that harmonizes skills, experience, and potential. In this chapter, we delve into the artistry of crafting questions that resonate with the unique cadence of diverse AI and ML roles – a symphony of inquiry that uncovers talents and aspirations.

The Art of Role Symphonies: Crafting the Overture

Imagine each role as a symphony, with its distinct melodies and harmonies. As you structure interview questions, picture yourself as the composer, penning the overture that sets the tone. Envision data scientist roles as sonatas of analytics, and machine learning engineer roles as concertos of model engineering. With each question, you create an anticipatory melody that draws candidates into their role's musical landscape.

Data Scientist: Unveiling the Sonata of Insights

Visualize data scientist roles as sonatas, where insights are the notes that unfold. In crafting questions, think of exploratory data analysis as the opening movement, where candidates dissect datasets like seasoned pianists interpreting musical scores. Envision hypothesis testing as a crescendo, unraveling the melodies of statistical significance. With each question, you unveil the sonata of a data scientist's narrative of discovery.

Machine Learning Engineer: Composing the Concerto of Models

Envision machine learning engineer roles as concertos, where models take center stage. Picture yourself as a conductor, orchestrating questions that showcase candidates' virtuosity in algorithm selection, hyperparameter tuning, and model evaluation. Think of ensemble techniques as harmonies that blend models' strengths. With each question, you compose a concerto that showcases their finesse in crafting predictive masterpieces.

AI Researcher: Envisioning the Symphony of Innovation

Imagine AI researcher roles as symphonies, where innovation is the crescendo that echoes through algorithms' corridors. As you structure questions, think of deep learning architectures as the movements that dance through neural networks. Envision reinforcement learning as the thematic thread that weaves agents and environments. With each question, you unravel the symphony of their research pursuits, harmonizing curiosity with groundbreaking potential.

Natural Language Processing Specialist: Crafting Dialogues of Understanding

Visualize NLP specialist roles as dialogues, where language is the medium of exploration. As you craft questions, think of tokenization as the lexicon that dissects words into phrases.

Envision word embeddings as the syntax that imbues words with semantic understanding. Picture named entity recognition as the discourse that identifies entities within text's narrative. With each question, you create a conversation that delves into their NLP proficiency.

Computer Vision Engineer: Picturing the Canvas of Perception

Think of computer vision engineer roles as canvases, where pixels and patterns paint the landscape of perception. Envision convolutional neural networks as brushes that capture local features with filters. Picture image segmentation as strokes that delineate objects' contours. Imagine object detection as the strokes that outline visual narratives. With each question, you paint a portrait of their ability to visualize and interpret the world through pixels.

Ethical AI Advocate: Chords of Humanity in the Symphony

Envision ethical AI roles as chords that resonate with the symphony of humanity. Think of fairness as the harmonious note that ensures just outcomes. Picture bias mitigation as the refrain that aligns predictions with values. Imagine privacy preservation as the melody that safeguards user trust. With each question, you compose an ethical symphony that underscores the importance of aligning AI's progress with human principles.

In this chapter, structuring interview questions for various AI and ML roles becomes a maestro's endeavor, where each question is a note that resonates with the essence of expertise. As you craft the symphony of inquiry, remember that you are not just an interviewer; you are a curator of potential, a conductor of aspirations, and a guardian of the symphony of AI and ML excellence across diverse roles.

B. Evaluating problem-solving and critical thinking skills

In the realm where algorithms unfurl the tapestry of intelligence and data casts its stories of insight, evaluating problem-solving and critical thinking skills becomes a pursuit that probes beyond the surface. Just as a detective deciphers clues to unravel mysteries, assessing these skills delves into the intricate workings of a candidate's cognitive symphony. In this chapter, we embark on a journey to master the art of evaluating problem-solving and critical thinking skills – a conductor's pursuit that unveils not just technical adeptness, but the orchestration of ingenuity and intellect.

The Symphony of Intellect: Unveiling Cognitive Mastery

Imagine problem-solving and critical thinking as a symphony, where notes of analysis, deduction, and innovation harmonize. In your role as a conductor, you orchestrate scenarios that invite candidates to showcase their virtuosity. Envision yourself as a maestro, guiding their cognitive crescendos to reveal the depth of their intellectual symphony.

Crafting the Puzzle: Setting the Stage for Ingenuity

Before candidates take the stage, envision yourself as a puzzle architect, designing enigmas that invite exploration. Think of coding challenges as pieces that fit into the puzzle, each one a fragment of problem-solving mastery. Picture yourself as a riddle maker, crafting scenarios that beckon candidates to unravel complexities with critical thinking acumen.

Analytical Agility: The Dance of Problem Decomposition

Envision problem decomposition as a dance, where candidates elegantly break down challenges into manageable steps. Think of this skill as a choreography, with each move representing their ability to dissect complexity. Imagine a candidate as a choreographer, transforming intricate routines of problems into graceful sequences of analytical agility.

Divergent Thinking: Embracing the Spectrum of Ideas

Imagine divergent thinking as a spectrum, where ideas radiate like hues of light. In your role as an assessor, envision yourself as a curator of creativity, gauging candidates' ability to explore multiple solutions. Think of brainstorming sessions as the canvas, where candidates paint their intellectual landscape with a palette of innovative possibilities.

Convergent Thinking: Harmonizing Ideas into Solutions

Envision convergent thinking as a symphony conductor, where ideas converge to form cohesive solutions. Picture candidates as composers, selecting harmonious notes from the cacophony of ideas. Think of algorithmic choices as musical compositions, where each selection resonates with the harmony of computational elegance.

Abductive Reasoning: Unraveling the Web of Hypotheses

Imagine abductive reasoning as a detective's web, where candidates untangle mysteries through inference. Visualize yourself as a sleuth, observing how candidates craft hypotheses that bridge gaps in knowledge. Think of this skill as a magnifying glass, zooming into the intricacies of their analytical prowess as they piece together fragments of evidence.

Scenario Analysis: Plotting Trajectories of Thought

Envision scenario analysis as a cartographer's chart, mapping trajectories of thought through complex terrain. Imagine candidates as explorers, navigating through hypothetical situations with astute judgment. Think of decision trees as their compass, guiding their choices along branches of logic that branch and converge, revealing the path of critical thought.

Innovative Solution Design: Orchestrating Ingenuity

Picture innovative solution design as a symphony conductor's baton, orchestrating notes of creativity into harmonious compositions. Envision candidates as composers of innovation, crafting solutions that blend elegance with effectiveness. Think of optimization techniques as your ensemble, refining their solutions into a symphony of ingenuity that resonates with both elegance and performance.

In this chapter, evaluating problem-solving and critical thinking skills becomes an odyssey of exploration, where each scenario, each code snippet, is a note in the symphony of intellectual prowess. As you guide candidates through this cognitive journey, remember that you are not just an assessor; you are an architect of insight, a conductor of cognitive symphonies, and a steward of the artistry that fuels innovation in the realm of AI and ML.

C. Assessing domain knowledge and practical applications

In the realm where algorithms converse with data and insights are extracted from digital terrain, assessing domain knowledge and practical applications becomes a voyage that bridges the chasm between theory and reality. Just as an explorer navigates uncharted territories, evaluating candidates' domain expertise is a journey that traverses the landscapes of knowledge and its tangible impact. In this chapter, we embark on a quest to master the art of assessing domain knowledge and practical applications – a navigator's endeavor that delves into the depths of specialization and the art of real-world orchestration.

The Atlas of Expertise: Navigating Domain Mastery

Imagine domain knowledge as an atlas, where each page is a realm of specialized insight waiting to be explored. In your role as a navigator, you chart the course through candidates' expertise, uncovering islands of knowledge and archipelagos of practical applications. Envision yourself as a cartographer, guiding the exploration of a candidate's cognitive cartography.

Crafting the Compass: Forging Pathways to Proficiency

Before candidates set sail, think of yourself as a compass maker, crafting questions that serve as guides to their domain knowledge. Envision situational scenarios as compass needles, pointing towards their practical compass of experience. Imagine case studies as constellations, illuminating their understanding of applying theoretical principles to real-world contexts.

The Elegance of Domain Fluency: Orchestrating Specialization

Picture domain fluency as a symphony, where candidates engage in a symphonic conversation with their specialized field. Envision yourself as a conductor, orchestrating questions that resonate with the nuances of their domain. Think of terminology as musical notes, each one contributing to the cadence of their expertise. As candidates respond, you uncover the symphony of their domain fluency.

Depth of Understanding: Delving into Layered Concepts

Imagine domain knowledge as a multi-layered narrative, with each layer revealing a deeper stratum of insight. Think of candidates as archaeologists, excavating layers of understanding through probing questions. Envision neural networks as a metaphor, where each question unravels another hidden layer of knowledge, exposing the depth of their comprehension.

Practical Applications: The Artistry of Real-World Fusion

Envision practical applications as the artisan's fusion of theory and reality, where candidates sculpt their knowledge into tangible creations. Picture yourself as a curator of case studies, inviting candidates to showcase their ability to transpose domain expertise into actionable strategies. Think of data-driven decision-making as a canvas, where candidates paint the strokes of practical wisdom.

Innovative Integration: The Symphony of Cross-Disciplinary Harmony

Imagine cross-disciplinary knowledge as a symphony, where domains harmonize to create innovative compositions. Envision candidates as conductors, orchestrating a symphony of fusion between AI and their specialized field. Think of ensemble techniques as the cadence that unites algorithms and domain knowledge, creating a harmonious synergy that resonates with innovative potential.

Real-World Problem-Solving: The Odyssey of Practical Impact

Visualize real-world problem-solving as an odyssey, where candidates embark on a quest to apply domain expertise to tangible challenges. Envision yourself as a questmaster, guiding candidates through scenarios that demand practical prowess. Think of optimization as their compass, steering their solutions towards the true north of impactful outcomes in the realm of AI and ML.

Ethical and Social Considerations: The Compass of Impactful Empathy

Picture ethical and social considerations as the compass that navigates domain knowledge towards responsible innovation. Envision candidates as guardians of impact, weighing their knowledge against the ethical implications of their actions. Think of fairness and accountability as the guideposts that steer their domain expertise towards a symphony of inclusive and ethically sound applications.

In this chapter, assessing domain knowledge and practical applications becomes a voyage of exploration, where each question, each scenario, is a coordinate in the cartography of expertise. As you guide candidates through this immersive journey, remember that you are not just an evaluator; you are a navigator of insights, a conductor of practical symphonies, and a steward of the artistry that bridges the gap between knowledge and its transformative impact in the domain of AI and ML.

CHAPTER 28

Behavioral Interview Techniques

In the vast expanse where algorithms meet human ingenuity, conducting interviews transcends the realm of technical prowess. Just as a playwright crafts characters that breathe life into a narrative, behavioral interview techniques unveil the intricate tapestry of candidates' experiences, values, and personalities. In this chapter, we embark on a journey to master the art of behavioral interview techniques – a playwright's pursuit that seeks not just skills, but the nuances of character, collaboration, and cultural fit.

The Theater of Experience: Unveiling the Narrative

Imagine each candidate as a protagonist, with their journey and experiences as the plotlines that weave their narrative. As an interviewer, you step onto the stage of insight, crafting questions that unveil the depth of their character. Envision yourself as a director, guiding candidates to perform their tales of challenges, triumphs, and growth.

Crafting the Dialogue: Setting the Stage for Authenticity

Before the interview unfolds, think of yourself as a scriptwriter, penning dialogues that invite candid self-expression. Envision scenario-based questions as scenes, where candidates step into the shoes of characters they've portrayed. Picture yourself as a dialogue coach, shaping interactions that evoke authenticity, allowing candidates to speak their truths on the stage of conversation.

Character Study: Unearthing Values and Motivations: Imagine character study as a psychological exploration, delving into candidates' motivations, values, and ethics. Envision yourself as an investigator, deciphering the psychological cues that reveal their perspectives. Picture decision-making scenarios as a magnifying glass, illuminating the underlying motivations that drive their behavioral scripts.

Collaborative Choreography: Assessing Team Dynamics

Envision collaborative skills as a dance, where candidates join the ensemble of a team. Think of teamwork scenarios as choreography, observing how candidates align their steps with others. Imagine conflict resolution as a duet, harmonizing differences into a synchronized performance. As you assess candidates' collaborative choreography, you uncover their ability to dance within the symphony of a team.

Adaptation Monologues: Navigating Change and Flexibility

Picture adaptation as a monologue, where candidates narrate their experiences in navigating change. Envision hypothetical challenges as scripts that prompt candidates to describe their responses to shifting scenarios. Think of change management as the script editing process, where candidates refine their monologues to reflect the harmony of resilience and flexibility.

Conflict Resolution: The Art of Harmonious Resolution

Imagine conflict resolution as a drama, where candidates showcase their ability to resolve tensions with grace. Envision role-play scenarios as scenes of negotiation, where candidates embody the protagonists of peaceful resolution. Picture empathy as the stage direction, guiding candidates to create a drama that culminates in the harmony of understanding.

Leadership Portraits: Portraitures of Influence and Impact

Visualize leadership scenarios as portraits, where candidates paint pictures of their influence and impact. Think of challenges as canvases, with candidates wielding the brush of leadership to shape outcomes. Envision effective communication as the palette, allowing candidates to blend colors of persuasion, motivation, and guidance.

Cultural Alignment: Casting for Cultural Fit

Envision cultural fit as a casting process, where candidates audition for roles that resonate with a company's ethos. Picture yourself as a casting director, evaluating how candidates align their values with the organization's culture. Think of cultural scenarios as scenes of camaraderie, where candidates harmonize their behavior with the cultural ensemble.

In this chapter, behavioral interview techniques become an art of character exploration, where each question, each scenario, is a glimpse into candidates' stories. As you direct candidates through this immersive journey, remember that you are not just an interviewer; you are a playwright of insight, a director of authenticity, and a guardian of the artistry that uncovers the nuances of character and collaboration in the grand theater of AI and ML.

A. Assessing teamwork and collaboration abilities

In the symphony of artificial intelligence and machine learning, where algorithms harmonize with human ingenuity, assessing teamwork and collaboration abilities becomes a symposium of shared expertise and collective brilliance. Just as a conductor orchestrates musicians to create harmonious melodies, evaluating candidates' teamwork skills uncovers the art of collaborative innovation. In this chapter, we embark on a journey to master the art of assessing teamwork and collaboration abilities – a conductor's endeavor that seeks not just individual talent, but the symphony of harmonious cooperation.

The Orchestra of Collaboration: Weaving a Collaborative Symphony

Imagine the interview room as a concert hall, where candidates join the orchestra of collaboration. As the conductor, you lead the ensemble, inviting candidates to play their parts in the symphony of team dynamics. Envision yourself as a maestro, guiding interactions that create a melody of shared expertise and unified efforts.

Crafting the Ensemble: Setting the Stage for Cooperation

Before the interview begins, think of yourself as a composer, crafting scenarios that invite candidates to join the collaborative ensemble. Envision group exercises as musical scores, where candidates harmonize their skills to create a collective masterpiece. Picture yourself as a choreographer, orchestrating movements that reveal the dance of teamwork and cooperation.

Harmony in Diversity: Embracing Multifaceted Dynamics

Imagine teamwork as a harmonious ensemble, where diverse skills and perspectives blend to create a resonant symphony.

Envision candidates as instruments, each contributing a unique timbre to the composition. Think of diversity as the spectrum of musical notes, each one enriching the collaborative melody with its distinct resonance.

Interplay of Roles: Observing Role Dynamics in Action

Envision role dynamics as a choreographed dance, where candidates step into roles that align with the collaborative choreography. Picture yourself as an audience member, observing how candidates execute their steps while complementing others. Think of role-switching scenarios as the change of movements, revealing their adaptability and ease in synchronizing with different parts of the ensemble.

Communication Cadence

Orchestrating Dialogues of Understanding: Imagine communication as a musical score, where candidates engage in dialogues that create harmonious understanding. Envision situational scenarios as script readings, where candidates articulate their thoughts and ideas to convey meaning. Think of active listening as the rhythmic pulse, guiding their conversations to a cadence of clear and effective communication.

Conflict Resolution: Navigating Harmonious Resolutions

Visualize conflict resolution as a duet, where candidates

collaborate to harmonize differences. Envision role-playing scenarios as scenes of negotiation, where candidates navigate tensions to create a harmonious resolution. Picture empathy as the key signature, guiding candidates to tune into each other's perspectives and reach a concordant resolution.

Shared Vision: Painting a Mural of Collaborative Goals

Imagine shared vision as a mural, where candidates contribute their strokes to create a collective masterpiece. Envision project-based questions as the canvas, where candidates paint their ideas and contributions to a common goal. Think of alignment as the brushstroke that ensures their individual efforts converge to create a unified image.

Cultural Contribution: Becoming a Note in the Cultural Symphony

Envision cultural fit as a musical note, where candidates add their resonance to the cultural symphony of the organization. Think of cultural scenarios as movements within a symphony, where candidates play their part while staying in harmony with the organization's ethos. Picture empathy as the tempo that guides their contributions to resonate with the cultural ensemble.

In this chapter, assessing teamwork and collaboration abilities becomes a symphony of shared expertise, where each interaction, each exercise, is a note in the collaborative composition. As you guide candidates through this orchestrated journey, remember that you are not just an assessor; you are a conductor of cohesion, a composer of cooperation, and a guardian of the artistry that underscores the power of collaborative innovation in the realm of AI and ML.

B. Adapting to dynamic and evolving AI projects

In the realm where algorithms evolve and data weaves narratives of change, adapting to dynamic and evolving AI projects becomes a dance of innovation and resilience. Just as a choreographer designs routines that flow with fluidity, navigating the ever-shifting landscape of AI projects requires a mastery of agility and creativity. In this chapter, we embark on a journey to master the art of adapting to dynamic and evolving AI projects – a choreographer's pursuit that seeks not just technical acumen, but the cadence of adaptation and the grace of transformation.

The Choreography of Adaptation: Crafting Seamless Transitions

Imagine AI projects as a choreographed dance, where each movement seamlessly transitions into the next. As a choreographer, you design routines that embrace change with grace. Envision yourself as a conductor of adaptation, guiding candidates to perform the steps that harmonize with the rhythm of evolving projects.

Crafting the Routine: Setting the Stage for Flexibility

Before candidates take the spotlight, think of yourself as a routine designer, creating scenarios that invite candidates to showcase their adaptability. Envision dynamic challenges as choreography that demands quick shifts in direction. Picture yourself as a coach, guiding candidates to execute routines that reflect the fluidity of their responses to change.

Innovation in Motion: Navigating Uncharted Territories

Imagine innovation as a choreographed solo, where candidates showcase their ability to navigate uncharted territories. Envision hypothetical scenarios as the stage, where candidates step into the spotlight and choreograph their unique responses to novel challenges. Think of creativity as the embellishment that adorns their routines with ingenuity and originality.

Agile Footwork: Swift Responses to Changing Tunes

Picture agile practices as the footwork that enables candidates to swiftly respond to changing tunes. Envision candidates as dancers who effortlessly adjust their steps to match the rhythm of evolving AI projects. Think of sprint cycles as dance routines, where candidates execute each step with precision and adapt their movements to the evolving choreography.

Collaborative Choreography: Synchronizing in the Dance of Change

Imagine collaboration as a duet, where candidates dance in synchronization with their team amidst change. Envision collaborative scenarios as partner routines, where candidates harmonize their steps to execute changes in tandem. Picture clear communication as the guiding hand that ensures each movement aligns with the evolving choreography.

Resilience as a Performance: Staying Graceful Amidst Challenges

Envision resilience as a solo performance, where candidates exhibit their ability to stay graceful amidst challenges. Think of past experiences as a repertoire of routines, each one demonstrating how candidates maintained poise in the face of adversity. Imagine resourcefulness as the improvisational flair that adds finesse to their performance of resilience.

Evolving Problem-Solving: Choreographing Solutions in Motion

Imagine problem-solving as an evolving choreography, where candidates choreograph solutions that adapt to changing contexts. Envision real-world challenges as stages, where candidates step into the limelight and perform their solutions amidst dynamic circumstances. Think of debugging as the art of refining their routines, ensuring seamless execution in the ever-evolving dance of AI projects.

Learning Choreography: Embracing the Art of Continuous Improvement

Picture continuous improvement as a learning choreography, where candidates embrace the art of refining their routines over time. Envision candidates as lifelong learners, rehearsing and revising their steps to achieve mastery. Think of retrospectives as the moments of reflection, where candidates analyze their performances and adjust their routines for a more polished dance.

In this chapter, adapting to dynamic and evolving AI projects becomes a dance of innovation and resilience, where each scenario, each challenge, is a step in the choreography of transformation. As you guide candidates through this rhythmic journey, remember that you are not just an assessor; you are a choreographer of adaptability, a conductor of innovation, and a guardian of the artistry that underscores the beauty of evolving projects in the realm of AI and ML.

C. Evaluating communication and problem-solving skills

In the realm where algorithms converse with insight and data bridges the gap between complexity and clarity, evaluating communication and problem-solving skills becomes a symphony of intellectual exchange and analytical finesse. Just as a conductor orchestrates a harmonious blend of instruments, assessing candidates' communication and problem-solving skills unveils the art of eloquence and the prowess of cognitive composition. In this chapter, we embark on a journey to master the art of evaluating communication and problem-solving skills – a conductor's pursuit that seeks not just technical prowess, but the cadence of clear expression and the precision of analytical acumen.

The Symphony of Dialogue: Crafting a Melody of Exchange

Imagine the interview room as a concert hall, where candidates engage in a symphony of dialogue. As the conductor, you guide the interaction, orchestrating a harmonious blend of questions and answers. Envision yourself as a maestro of communication, conducting candidates through a symphony of expressive exchange.

Crafting the Conversation: Setting the Stage for Clarity

Before candidates step onto the stage, think of yourself as a playwright, scripting dialogues that invite candidates to communicate with clarity. Envision scenario-based questions as scenes, where candidates articulate their thoughts as characters in the narrative. Picture yourself as a director, guiding candidates to deliver their lines with eloquence and precision.

Art of Explanation: Painting Concepts with Verbal Brushstrokes

Imagine the art of explanation as a canvas, where candidates paint abstract concepts with vivid verbal brushstrokes. Envision candidates as artists, using language to craft a vivid picture that clarifies intricate notions. Think of metaphorical expression as the palette, allowing candidates to blend shades of analogy to illuminate complex ideas.

Analytical Sonnets: Composing Solutions with Precision

Picture problem-solving as the composition of analytical sonnets, where candidates craft elegant solutions with precise structures. Envision hypothetical challenges as poetic verses, where candidates rhyme their thought process with the rhythm of analysis. Think of data-driven deductions as the poetic meter, guiding candidates to construct solutions with poetic precision.

Socratic Dialogue: Navigating Complex Terrain with Grace

Imagine Socratic dialogue as a journey through complex landscapes, where candidates traverse intricate terrains with grace. Envision thought-provoking questions as milestones, prompting candidates to embark on a philosophical exploration. Think of probing inquiries as the compass, steering candidates through the labyrinth of intricate reasoning.

Collaborative Dialogues: Weaving Discourse in a Team Ensemble

Visualize collaborative communication as a duet, where candidates engage in harmonious discourse within a team ensemble. Envision collaborative scenarios as shared dialogues, where candidates interweave their ideas and viewpoints. Picture active listening as the syncopated rhythm, guiding candidates to respond and harmonize with their teammates' contributions.

Scenario Narratives: Unfolding Solutions in Verbal Storytelling

Imagine scenario narratives as verbal storytelling, where candidates unfold solutions as intricate tales. Envision real-world challenges as the narrative arc, where candidates captivate with their storytelling prowess. Think of contextualization as the plot device, guiding candidates to set the stage and immerse the audience in the narrative of their problem-solving journey.

Conversational Adaptation: Adjusting Discourse to Audience Cadence

Picture conversational adaptation as a dance of dialogue, where candidates adjust their discourse to match the cadence of the audience. Envision candidates as conversationalists who elegantly modulate their communication style. Think of adapting language complexity as the dance choreography, ensuring that candidates tailor their message for a harmonious interaction.

In this chapter, evaluating communication and problem-solving skills becomes a symphony of intellectual discourse, where each question, each answer, is a note in the composition of insight. As you conduct candidates through this expressive journey, remember that you are not just an evaluator; you are a conductor of clarity, a curator of coherence, and a guardian of the artistry that underpins the beauty of communication and problem-solving in the grand symphony of AI and ML.

CHAPTER 29

Creating a Positive Interview Experience

In the theater of talent acquisition, where aspirations take center stage and potential unfurls its wings, creating a positive interview experience becomes a masterpiece of hospitality and empathy. Just as a host welcomes guests into a sanctuary of comfort, designing an interview experience that resonates with positivity and respect is akin to crafting a symphony of connection and mutual understanding. In this chapter, we embark on a journey to master the art of creating a positive interview experience – a host's endeavor that seeks not just evaluation, but the orchestration of rapport and the cultivation of an environment where candidates shine as the stars of their own narrative.

The Gallery of First Impressions: A Canvas of Warmth and Welcome

Imagine the interview setting as a gallery, where candidates step onto the canvas of their potential. As the curator, you design an environment that exudes warmth and welcome. Envision yourself as an artist of hospitality, painting the backdrop of their first impressions with strokes of genuine kindness and attentiveness.

Crafting the Atmosphere: Setting the Stage for Comfort

Before candidates arrive, think of yourself as an interior decorator, arranging elements that envelop candidates in a cocoon of ease. Envision the interview room as a haven, where candidates feel at ease to showcase their true selves. Picture yourself as a conductor of comfort, orchestrating an ambiance that encourages candid expression.

Empathetic Choreography: Dancing in the Footsteps of Candidate's Journey

Imagine empathy as a choreography, where candidates step into the spotlight of their journey. Envision each question as a dance step, leading candidates through a sequence that resonates with their experiences. Think of your role as the dance partner, mirroring their emotions and guiding the rhythm of conversation.

Personalized Narratives: Weaving a Tale Tailored to Aspirations

Picture personalized interview narratives as bespoke garments, tailored to candidates' aspirations and dreams. Envision candidates as the protagonists, and each question as a chapter that unravels their story. Think of your role as the narrative weaver, guiding candidates to share their tales of achievements, passions, and ambitions.

Constructive Feedback: An Art of Nurturing Growth

Imagine constructive feedback as a sculptor's chisel, shaping candidates' potential with precision. Envision feedback as an art form, sculpting paths for improvement and growth. Think of your role as the artisan, crafting insights that foster development and empower candidates on their journey towards excellence.

Responsive Communication: A Symphony of Timely Engagement

Visualize responsive communication as a symphony, where candidates' inquiries are met with harmonious engagement. Envision each interaction as a musical note, playing in rhythm to candidates' queries. Think of prompt responses as the tempo that guides the flow of conversation and nurtures a sense of importance.

Transparency and Authenticity: Painting a Portrait of Truthfulness

Picture transparency as a portrait, where candidates perceive an authentic depiction of the opportunity. Envision your role as the portrait artist, capturing the essence of the role, its challenges, and the organizational culture. Think of authenticity as the brush that strokes candid conversations and fosters mutual trust.

Farewell as a Continuation: Nurturing Relationships Beyond the Interview

Imagine the end of the interview as a curtain call, where candidates prepare to exit the stage. Envision farewells as a promise, a continuation of a relationship nurtured beyond the interview. Think of your role as the custodian of connections, ensuring that the closing moments resonate with warmth and enthusiasm for future interactions.

In this chapter, creating a positive interview experience becomes a masterpiece of rapport and hospitality, where each interaction, each question, is a stroke in the canvas of connection. As you orchestrate candidates through this experiential journey, remember that you are not just an interviewer; you are a host of harmony, a guardian of goodwill, and a maestro of moments that elevate the interview experience into a symphony of positivity in the realm of AI and ML.

A. Providing clear expectations and guidance

In the realm where algorithms decipher intricacies and data illuminates paths, providing clear expectations and guidance becomes a compass that guides candidates through the labyrinth of possibility. Just as a navigator charts a course through uncharted waters, offering candidates a clear roadmap ensures their journey is infused with purpose and direction. In this chapter, we embark on a journey to master the art of providing clear expectations and guidance – a navigator's pursuit that seeks not just orientation, but the harmonious blend of clarity and empowerment.

The Cartography of Clarity: Mapping a Trail of Understanding

Imagine the interview process as a terrain waiting to be explored. As the cartographer, you design a map that navigates candidates through the landscape of expectation. Envision yourself as a navigator, equipping candidates with a compass of understanding to traverse the challenges and opportunities that lie ahead.

Crafting the Compass: Setting the Stage for Direction

Before candidates begin their journey, think of yourself as a trailblazer, creating signposts that illuminate the path. Envision instructions and guidelines as guideposts, leading candidates towards their destination with ease. Picture yourself as a tour guide, offering a compass of insight to help candidates confidently navigate each step.

Narrating the Expedition: Charting Each Milestone with Precision

Imagine the interview stages as chapters in an unfolding

narrative. Envision each milestone as a plot point, guiding candidates through the plot of their journey. Think of your role as the narrator, articulating the purpose of each stage with clarity and context, creating a sense of anticipation and engagement.

Structured Scenario Exploration: Navigating Through Hypothetical Realities

Picture structured scenarios as intriguing landscapes waiting to be explored. Envision hypothetical challenges as immersive settings where candidates journey to test their skills. Think of your role as the scenario architect, creating vivid environments that encourage candidates to showcase their abilities and problem-solving prowess.

Expectation Roadmap: Defining Milestones Along the Way

Imagine an expectation roadmap as a series of milestones that mark candidates' progress. Envision checkpoints as signifiers of achievement, guiding candidates toward their ultimate destination. Think of your role as the signpost designer, placing markers that signify their advancement and motivate their pursuit.

Resourceful Navigation: Equipping Candidates for Journey Success

Visualize resourceful navigation as providing explorers with the tools they need. Envision resources as supplies that empower candidates to traverse challenges with confidence. Think of your role as the supplier, ensuring candidates are equipped with the knowledge, materials, and support to navigate successfully.

Constructive Feedback as a Compass of Improvement

Imagine constructive feedback as a compass that points candidates towards growth. Envision feedback sessions as rest stops where candidates recalibrate their trajectory. Think of your role as the feedback guide, steering candidates toward areas of improvement while offering encouragement and direction.

Engagement and Communication: A Beacon of Guided Interaction

Picture engagement and communication as a lighthouse that illuminates candidates' way. Envision regular updates as the lighthouse beam that keeps candidates informed and engaged. Think of your role as the lighthouse keeper, ensuring candidates never lose sight of their progress and the broader journey.

In this chapter, providing clear expectations and guidance becomes a navigational symphony, where each directive, each milestone, is a note in the composition of candidate empowerment. As you guide candidates through this orchestrated journey, remember that you are not just a guide; you are a cartographer of confidence, a trailblazer of transparency, and a guardian of the artistry that shapes the journey's clarity and empowerment in the realm of AI and ML.

B. Cultivating a fair and respectful interview process

In the realm where algorithms seek fairness and data reflects integrity, cultivating a fair and respectful interview process becomes a garden of equality and professionalism. Just as a gardener tends to each plant with care, nurturing an interview process that upholds principles of fairness and respect is akin to cultivating a landscape where every candidate's potential can flourish. In this chapter, we embark on a journey to master the art of cultivating a fair and respectful interview process – a gardener's endeavor that seeks not just assessment, but the blooming of inclusivity and the fragrance of ethical conduct.

The Garden of Equity: Nurturing a Tapestry of Inclusion

Imagine the interview process as a vibrant garden, where each candidate's uniqueness is a colorful bloom. As the gardener, you tend to the garden of equity, ensuring that each candidate is given the opportunity to grow and shine. Envision yourself as a steward of diversity, planting seeds of inclusivity and tending to the soil of unbiased evaluation.

Cultivating Professional Soil: Creating a Bedrock of Respect

Before candidates enter the garden, think of yourself as a soil preparer, cultivating a foundation of respect and professionalism. Envision interview guidelines as garden boundaries, where respect for candidates' time, opinions, and experiences is the fertile soil in which their potential thrives. Picture yourself as a landscaper, sculpting an environment where every candidate is treated with honor.

Tending to Fair Assessment: Ushering Each Flower to Bloom

Imagine fair assessment as a sunbeam that nourishes each blossom equally. Envision evaluation criteria as sunlight, illuminating candidates' achievements and capabilities without casting shadows of bias. Think of your role as the sunlight distributor, ensuring that each candidate's strengths are showcased, irrespective of background or origin.

Rooted in Ethical Conduct: Uplifting Each Candidate's Experience

Picture ethical conduct as the root system that supports the garden of fairness and respect. Envision ethical guidelines as sturdy roots that hold the process upright and ensure it remains grounded in integrity. Think of your role as the gardener's caretaker, maintaining a nurturing environment where candidates feel valued and secure.

Harvesting Inclusive Questions: Crafting Buds of Universality

Imagine inclusive questions as buds that blossom into understanding and insight. Envision question crafting as nurturing, ensuring that every query remains free from bias and encourages a diverse range of responses. Think of your role as the question gardener, planting seeds of universality that invite candidates to share their perspectives authentically.

Pruning Bias: Trimming Away Discrimination and Stereotypes

Visualize pruning bias as an essential step to ensure the garden of fairness remains unmarred. Envision bias identification as a gardener's pruning shears, trimming away discriminatory language and stereotypes that may inadvertently creep into the process. Think of your role as the guardian of purity, ensuring the interview environment remains untainted by preconceived notions.

Cultivating Feedback: Nurturing Growth with Constructive Insight

Imagine feedback as nourishment that helps candidates

flourish. Envision feedback sessions as moments of care, where candidates receive insights to cultivate their potential. Think of your role as the gardener's advisor, providing guidance that fosters growth, resilience, and continuous improvement.

A Bouquet of Respect: Parting Ways with Dignity

Picture the end of the interview process as a bouquet of respect presented to each candidate. Envision post-interview interactions as the gentle handing of the bouquet, symbolizing appreciation for candidates' time and efforts. Think of your role as the bouquet bearer, ensuring that each candidate leaves with a sense of value and dignity.

In this chapter, cultivating a fair and respectful interview process becomes a horticultural symphony, where each interaction, each question, is a note in the composition of an inclusive and ethical environment. As you tend to candidates through this nurtured journey, remember that you are not just an interviewer; you are a gardener of equality, a curator of professionalism, and a guardian of the artistry that underlies the flourishing garden of fairness and respect in the realm of AI and ML.

C. Constructive feedback and improvement suggestions

In the realm where algorithms refine and data refines,

constructive feedback and improvement suggestions become tools of growth, chiseling candidates into polished gems of potential. Just as a sculptor shapes raw material into exquisite art, providing feedback that nurtures improvement is akin to sculpting each candidate's capabilities into brilliance. In this chapter, we embark on a journey to master the art of delivering constructive feedback and improvement suggestions – a craftsman's pursuit that seeks not just assessment, but the honing of skills and the evolution of excellence.

The Sculptor's Workshop: Crafting Growth with Insight

Imagine the interview process as a sculptor's workshop, where each candidate's abilities are honed and refined. As the sculptor, you wield feedback as your chisel, shaping raw potential into masterpieces of improvement. Envision yourself as an artisan of growth, guiding candidates through the intricate process of skill refinement.

The Canvas of Constructive Insight: Brushing Strokes of Progress

Before candidates step into the workshop, think of yourself as a painter, delicately applying strokes of constructive insight. Envision feedback sessions as the canvas on which candidates' progress is painted with precision. Picture yourself as a curator of critique, offering a palette of guidance that blends both affirmation and areas for development.

Sculpting Strengths: Carving a Path to Excellence

Imagine sculpting strengths as chiseling away the excess to reveal candidates' inherent talents. Envision feedback as the sculptor's chisel, shaping candidates' strong points into refined contours of excellence. Think of your role as the craftsman, carefully carving away distractions to uncover the true brilliance that lies beneath.

Polishing Rough Edges: Smoothing the Path to Refinement

Picture polishing rough edges as sanding away imperfections, revealing candidates' true potential. Envision feedback as the artisan's sandpaper, smoothing out areas that require refinement. Think of your role as the polisher, tirelessly working to eliminate distractions and inconsistencies, allowing candidates to shine more brilliantly.

Personalized Artistry: Tailoring Feedback to Growth Trajectories

Imagine personalized artistry as custom-fit attire that accentuates candidates' progress. Envision feedback sessions as fitting rooms, where candidates try on tailored insights that suit their growth journey. Think of your role as the designer, creating bespoke improvement plans that address individual needs and aspirations.

Balancing Warmth and Precision: Delivering Feedback with Grace

Picture balancing warmth and precision as a dance of diplomacy, where feedback is presented with care. Envision feedback delivery as a ballet of expression, where candidates are guided through areas of improvement with grace. Think of your role as the choreographer, ensuring that each step is taken thoughtfully, respecting candidates' efforts.

An Elevation of Perspective: Shaping Vistas of Enhancement

Imagine feedback as a viewpoint that elevates candidates' understanding of their performance. Envision feedback sessions as the ascent to a higher vantage point, offering candidates new perspectives on their capabilities. Think of your role as the guide, leading candidates to vistas of insight that inspire them to strive for continuous improvement.

Empowerment Through Suggestions: Planting Seeds of Progress

Picture improvement suggestions as seeds that candidates can nurture into growth. Envision feedback as a gardening process, where each suggestion is a seed that, with care, can blossom into progress. Think of your role as the gardener, planting these seeds with candidates, and providing the nurturing guidance required for them to flourish.

In this chapter, delivering constructive feedback and improvement suggestions becomes an artistic symphony, where each insight, each suggestion, is a note in the composition of candidate enhancement. As you sculpt candidates through this crafted journey, remember that you are not just a feedback provider; you are a sculptor of potential, a curator of progress, and a guardian of the artistry that underpins the growth and evolution in the realm of AI and ML.

Conclusion

As we draw the final curtain on this journey through these pages, we invite you to reflect on the knowledge, insights, and discoveries that have unfolded before you. Our exploration of various subjects has been a captivating voyage into the depths of understanding.

In these chapters, we have ventured through the intricacies of numerous topics and examined the key concepts and findings that define these fields. It is our hope that you have found inspiration, enlightenment, and valuable takeaways that resonate with you on your own quest for knowledge.

Remember that the pursuit of understanding is an ever-evolving journey, and this book is but a milestone along the way. The world of knowledge is vast and boundless, offering endless opportunities for exploration and growth.

As you conclude this book, we encourage you to carry forward the torch of curiosity and continue your exploration of these subjects. Seek out new perspectives, engage in meaningful discussions, and embrace the thrill of lifelong learning.

We express our sincere gratitude for joining us on this intellectual adventure. Your curiosity and dedication to expanding your horizons are the driving forces behind our shared quest for wisdom and insight.

Thank you for entrusting us with a portion of your intellectual journey. May your pursuit of knowledge lead you to new heights and inspire others to embark on their own quests for understanding.

With profound gratitude,

Nikhilesh Mishra, Author

Glossary of Terms

Artificial Intelligence (AI): The field of computer science focused on creating intelligent agents capable of mimicking human cognitive functions such as learning, reasoning, problem-solving, and decision-making.

Machine Learning (ML): A subset of AI that involves the development of algorithms and models that enable computers to learn from and make predictions or decisions based on data.

Neural Network: A computational model inspired by the structure and function of the human brain, consisting of interconnected nodes that process information and learn patterns from data.

Data Preprocessing: The process of cleaning, transforming, and organizing raw data into a suitable format for analysis, improving the quality and reliability of subsequent results.

Feature Engineering: The process of selecting, transforming, or creating relevant features from the raw data to enhance the performance of machine learning algorithms.

Algorithm: A set of step-by-step instructions or rules followed by a computer to solve a specific problem or perform a task.

Expert Systems: AI systems that encode human expertise and knowledge into software to solve complex problems.

Data Transformation: Converting data from one format or structure to another, often to improve compatibility or facilitate analysis.

Data Cleaning: The process of identifying and correcting errors, inconsistencies, or inaccuracies in a dataset.

Scaling: Rescaling variables to have a consistent scale or range, often to ensure fair comparison in algorithms.

Principal Component Analysis (PCA): A dimensionality reduction technique used to transform high-dimensional data into a lower-dimensional representation while retaining essential information.

Missing Values: Data points that are absent or not recorded in a dataset.

Outliers: Data points that significantly deviate from the expected patterns in a dataset.

Z-Score: A statistical measure used to identify outliers by measuring how many standard deviations a data point is from the mean.

Box Plot: A graphical representation used to display the distribution, central tendency, and variability of data.

Supervised Learning: A type of machine learning where the algorithm learns patterns from labeled data to make predictions or decisions.

Unsupervised Learning: A type of machine learning where the algorithm identifies patterns in unlabeled data, such as clustering and dimensionality reduction.

Reinforcement Learning: A type of machine learning where an agent learns to make decisions through interactions with an environment to maximize rewards.

Deep Learning: A subset of machine learning that involves neural networks with multiple layers, enabling the model to learn intricate patterns and representations.

Convolutional Neural Network (CNN): A type of neural network designed for image analysis and recognition.

Recurrent Neural Network (RNN): A type of neural network capable of processing sequences of data, making it suitable for tasks like natural language processing.

Natural Language Processing (NLP): The branch of AI that focuses on enabling computers to understand, interpret, and generate human language.

Tokenization: The process of splitting text into smaller units, such as words or phrases, for analysis.

API (Application Programming Interface): A set of protocols and tools that allows different software applications to communicate and interact with each other.

Bias in AI: Unintentional or systemic prejudices that can be present in AI models due to biased training data.

AI Winter: Periods of reduced funding and interest in AI research due to technological limitations and unfulfilled expectations.

Information Processing: The manipulation, organization, and transformation of data to extract meaningful insights.

Data Imputation: Filling in missing values in a dataset using various techniques.

Exploratory Data Analysis (EDA): The process of visually and quantitatively summarizing and understanding the main characteristics of a dataset.

Hyperparameters: Parameters set before training a model that influence its behavior, such as learning rate and regularization strength.

Model Evaluation: The process of assessing the performance and quality of machine learning models using various metrics and techniques.

Overfitting: A situation where a model learns the training data too well, capturing noise and hindering its ability to generalize to new data.

Model Deployment: The process of integrating a trained machine learning model into a production environment to make real-time predictions.

Ethics in AI: The evaluation of potential moral, social, and cultural implications of AI and machine learning applications.

Quantum Computing: Advanced computing technology that uses quantum bits (qubits) to perform complex calculations, potentially revolutionizing AI and ML.

Transfer Learning: A technique where a pre-trained model is adapted to a new, related task, often resulting in improved performance with less training data.

Explainable AI (XAI): The effort to make AI models and their decisions interpretable and understandable by humans.

Generative Adversarial Networks (GANs): A class of AI models where two networks, a generator and a discriminator, compete to produce realistic outputs.

Business Intelligence (BI): The use of data analysis tools and techniques to gather insights and make informed decisions in business operations.

Predictive Analytics: The use of historical data and statistical algorithms to predict future outcomes and trends in business.

Virtual Reality (VR): A simulated environment that can be experienced through a computer-generated interface, often used for entertainment purposes.

Augmented Reality (AR): A technology that overlays digital information onto the real world, enhancing the user's perception and interaction.

Smart Assistants: Voice-activated AI applications that can perform tasks, provide information, and assist users in various daily activities.

Internet of Things (IoT): A network of interconnected physical devices and objects embedded with sensors and software to exchange data.

Bias-Variance Tradeoff: The balance between a model's ability to fit the training data (low bias) and its ability to generalize to new, unseen data (low variance).

Cross-Validation: A technique used to assess the performance of a model by partitioning the data into subsets for training and testing.

Ensemble Learning: The process of combining multiple models to improve overall performance and robustness.

Gradient Descent: An optimization algorithm used to minimize the error of a model by adjusting its parameters iteratively.

Regularization: Techniques applied to prevent overfitting by adding constraints to the model's parameters.

Precision and Recall: Metrics used to evaluate the performance of classification models, especially in imbalanced datasets.

ROC Curve: A graphical representation of a model's performance across different classification thresholds.

K-Means Clustering: An unsupervised learning algorithm used to partition data points into clusters based on similarity.

Natural Language Generation: The process of generating human-readable text using AI models.

Artificial General Intelligence (AGI): AI that possesses human-like cognitive abilities and can understand, learn, and apply knowledge across a wide range of tasks.

Swarm Intelligence: A collective behavior exhibited by decentralized systems, often inspired by the behavior of social organisms.

Adversarial Attacks: Techniques used to exploit vulnerabilities in machine learning models by introducing carefully crafted input data.

Unstructured Data: Data that doesn't have a specific format or structure, often including text, images, audio, and video.

Resources and References

As you reach the final pages of this book by Nikhilesh Mishra, consider it not an ending but a stepping stone. The pursuit of knowledge is an unending journey, and the world of information is boundless.

Discover a World Beyond These Pages

We extend a warm invitation to explore a realm of boundless learning and discovery through our dedicated online platform: **www.nikhileshmishra.com**. Here, you will unearth a carefully curated trove of resources and references to empower your quest for wisdom.

Unleash the Potential of Your Mind

- **Digital Libraries:** Immerse yourself in vast digital libraries, granting access to books, research papers, and academic treasures.

- **Interactive Courses:** Engage with interactive courses and lectures from world-renowned institutions, nurturing your thirst for knowledge.

- **Enlightening Talks:** Be captivated by enlightening talks delivered by visionaries and experts from diverse fields.

- **Community Connections:** Connect with a global community of like-minded seekers, engage in meaningful discussions, and share your knowledge journey.

Your Journey Has Just Begun

Your journey as a seeker of knowledge need not end here. Our website awaits your exploration, offering a gateway to an infinite universe of insights and references tailored to ignite your intellectual curiosity..

Acknowledgments

As I stand at this pivotal juncture, reflecting upon the completion of this monumental work, I am overwhelmed with profound gratitude for the exceptional individuals who have been instrumental in shaping this remarkable journey.

In Loving Memory

To my father, **Late Shri Krishna Gopal Mishra,** whose legacy of wisdom and strength continues to illuminate my path, even in his physical absence, I offer my deepest respect and heartfelt appreciation.

The Pillars of Support

My mother, **Mrs. Vijay Kanti Mishra,** embodies unwavering resilience and grace. Your steadfast support and unwavering faith in my pursuits have been the bedrock of my journey.

To my beloved wife, **Mrs. Anshika Mishra,** your unshakable belief in my abilities has been an eternal wellspring of motivation. Your constant encouragement has propelled me to reach new heights.

My daughter, **Miss Aarvi Mishra,** infuses my life with boundless joy and unbridled inspiration. Your insatiable curiosity serves as a constant reminder of the limitless power of exploration and discovery.

Brothers in Arms

To my younger brothers, **Mr. Ashutosh Mishra** and **Mr. Devashish Mishra,** who have steadfastly stood by my side, offering unwavering support and shared experiences that underscore the strength of familial bonds.

A Journey Shared

This book is a testament to the countless hours of dedication and effort that have gone into its creation. I am immensely grateful for the privilege of sharing my knowledge and insights with a global audience.

Readers, My Companions

To all the readers who embark on this intellectual journey alongside me, your curiosity and unquenchable thirst for knowledge inspire me to continually push the boundaries of understanding in the realm of cloud computing.

With profound appreciation and sincere gratitude,

Nikhilesh Mishra

August 18, 2023

About the Author

Nikhilesh Mishra is an extraordinary visionary, propelled by an insatiable curiosity and an unyielding passion for innovation. With a relentless commitment to exploring the boundaries of knowledge and technology, Nikhilesh has embarked on an exceptional journey to unravel the intricate complexities of our world.

Hailing from the vibrant and diverse landscape of India, Nikhilesh's pursuit of knowledge has driven him to plunge deep into the world of discovery and understanding from a remarkably young age. His unwavering determination and quest for innovation have not only cemented his position as a thought leader but have also earned him global recognition in the ever-evolving realm of technology and human understanding.

Over the years, Nikhilesh has not only mastered the art of translating complex concepts into accessible insights but has also crafted a unique talent for inspiring others to explore the limitless possibilities of human potential.

Nikhilesh's journey transcends the mere boundaries of expertise; it is a transformative odyssey that challenges conventional wisdom and redefines the essence of exploration. His commitment to pushing the boundaries and reimagining the norm serves as a luminous beacon of inspiration to all those who aspire to make a profound impact in the world of knowledge.

As you navigate the intricate corridors of human understanding and innovation, you will not only gain insight into Nikhilesh's expertise but also experience his unwavering dedication to empowering readers like you. Prepare to be enthralled as he seamlessly melds intricate insights with real-world applications, igniting the flames of curiosity and innovation within each reader.

Nikhilesh Mishra's work extends beyond the realm of authorship; it is a reflection of his steadfast commitment to shaping the future of knowledge and exploration. It is an embodiment of his boundless dedication to disseminating wisdom for the betterment of individuals worldwide.

Prepare to be inspired, enlightened, and empowered as you embark on this transformative journey alongside Nikhilesh Mishra. Your understanding of the world will be forever enriched, and your passion for exploration and innovation will reach new heights under his expert guidance.

Sincerely, **A Fellow Explorer**

Notes

Notes

Notes

Notes

www.ingramcontent.com/pod-product-compliance
Lightning Source LLC
LaVergne TN
LVHW051426050326
832903LV00030BD/2946